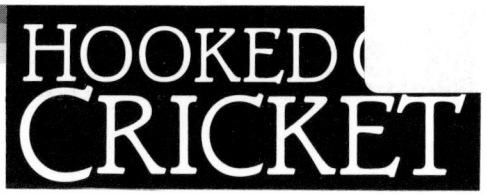

MAX WALKER is one of Australia's greatest and most-loved sporting characters. After an auspicious Australian Rules and Test cricket career, the 'Tangles' legend has spread even further, to every household in Australia, with his witty TV sports presenting, hilarious after-dinner speeches and lively writings.

The tall Tasmanian, who bowled with the famous tangle-footed approach, developed a tremendous empathy with cricket spectators and sports fans on grounds all over the world. The Melbourne Cricket Ground's 'Bay 13' fans adopted him as their favourite son, a status he still enjoys today.

Hooked on Cricket is an entertaining romp, a cricket addict's A to Z guide, full of anecdotes about Max's much-loved cricketing life, the tremendous characters he has met along the way, combined with some serious advice for the next generation of cricketing stars.

Max has adopted a *Boys' Own Annual* approach to this book and includes a potpourri of cricketing material which will delight both new and established cricketing fans. The older generation will revel in the tales of Doug Walters, Dennis Lillee and other Test legends while younger readers will enjoy the quizzes, instructions and the good sense which makes 'Mr Walker' such a charismatic name in Australian sporting circles.

KEN PIESSE is a keen club cricketer and freelance journalist who has edited Australia's national cricket magazine, *Cricketer*, since 1978. He is a great Max Walker fan, despite suffering the indignity of Walker hoiking several of his best social-match leg breaks one bounce over the long-on boundary into the MCG's Southern Stand.

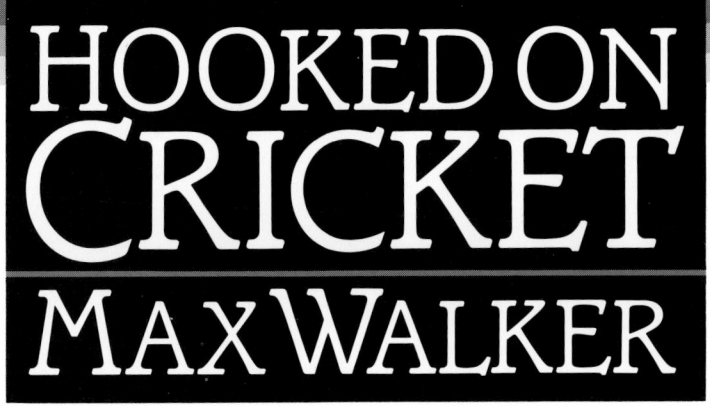

AN ADDICT'S A-Z GUIDE

With Ken Piesse

M

Copyright © Max Walker Promotions 1989

All rights reserved.
No part of this publication
may be reproduced or transmitted,
in any form or by any means,
without permission.

First published 1989 by
THE MACMILLAN COMPANY OF AUSTRALIA PTY LTD
107 Moray Street, South Melbourne 3205
6 Clarke Street, Crows Nest 2065
Reprinted 1989

Associated companies and representatives
throughout the world.

National Library of Australia
cataloguing in publication data

Walker, Max, 1948– .
  Hooked on cricket, an addict's a-z guide

  Bibliography.
  ISBN 0 333 50161 6

  1. Walker, Max, 1948– . –Anecdotes. 2. Cricket –
  Australia–Anecdotes. I. Piesse, Ken. II. Title.

796.35'8'0924

Set in 11pt Century Old Style, edited and formatted on the
Apple Macintosh Plus from author's disks and output to the
Linotronic 300 at On the Ball Computer Resource Centre, 265
Coventry Street, South Melbourne, 3205.

Printed in Australia by Globe Press Pty Ltd

Contents

INTRODUCTION: 'AVE A GO, YER MUG!	vii
BATTING	xi
BOWLING	xii
FIELDING	xiii
'A.B.' TAKES A WRONG TURN; CROCODILE DOUGIE BITES 'CHAPPELLI'	1
AUSTRALIAN XI PLAYERS TO HEAD ENGLISH FIRST-CLASS AVERAGES	2
BEFORE YOU EAT THAT ORANGE…	3
BE IN CONTROL AT ALL TIMES	4
BOTTOMS UP!	7
BRADMAN AND THE GREATS	8
CAN LITTLE JOHNNY RING HOME? HIS MOTHER IS WORRIED	10
CAUGHT ON A STICKY	11
COLOUR CRICKET — VIA THE RADIO	12
COPYCATS (OR, HOW TO IMPROVE YOURSELF BY WATCHING OTHERS)	13
DAY OF THE DOODLEBUG (OR, THE FASTEST BALL I EVER FACED)	17
DOING THE QUICKSTEP	18
EXCUSE ME MISTER, CAN I HAVE YOUR AUTOGRAPH?	19
FANCY A BOWL?; FINE TUNING YOUR SKILLS	22
GOT PROBLEMS? HIT THEM HEAD ON!	28
HAPPY SNAPS	29
HOW TO GET AUTOGRAPHS WHEN THE TEAMS ARE OUT OF TOWN	32
HOW TO MULTIPLY YOUR BATTING AVERAGE BY FOUR	33
HOW TO STOP A 'STEAM TRAIN'	36
'I'M GOING TO ENGLAND TO PLAY CRICKET, NOT SIGN #$¿¡%@ AUTOGRAPHS!'	40
'JOHNNY WON'T HIT TODAY' AND OTHER GREAT ONE-LINERS	42
KANGA CRICKET — IT'S FUN BUT…	44
LEGENDS AND HOW THEY START	46
MAGIC MOMENTS (FASTEST TEST 100S; MOST RUNS OFF A TEST OVER)	48
MEMORIES OF MY FIRST TEST INNINGS	50
MY MOST EMBARRASSING MOMENT	51
NICE GUYS DO WIN	53
NICKNAMES AND WHY THEY CALL ME 'TANGLES'; NO ONE WANTED TO BAT	54
OOPS! I FAIL TO RECOGNISE 'THE DON'	56
PRANKS FROM DOUGIE AND OTHER CRICKETERS OF MY TIME	57

Queen's Park and an unforgettable victory	59
'Redders' and my favourite bat	63
Self-made champions	68
Schooldays	69
Shorten the pitch!; Stars-talk	70
Start 'em young; Superstitions	73
Some 'Shark'-like theory	74
Tales of 'Tiny', Big Wes and 'Fiery' Boycott	75
'Tang, we need a wicket'	77
Ten tall tales but true	79
The best centuries I've seen	82
The best techniques I know (batting; bowling)	84
The 'done' thing and why players should behave	85
The greatest team I ever played against	85
The most valuable lesson I ever learnt	88
The truth about 'Chappelli' and the Coke bottle	88
Twisters from Tangles	91
Ugly scenes at the MCG and other commentary classics	96
Unforgettable moments	99
Veletta and some fielding theory	101
Watch and win; What's wrong with competing?	105
Whoops, I've broken a window!	106
Why eight-ball overs are a must	107
XXXX cricket (or, the most amazing batting collapse I've seen)	108
You can't score runs sitting in the pavilion	110
Your day at the cricket	111
Zootas, flippers and bunnies	114
Acknowledgements and Bibliography	118
Appendix: Max Walker — for the record (statistics; opinions)	119

Introduction
'Ave a go, yer mug!

SO YOU love cricket! Isn't it marvellous? Once bitten, you're an addict for life. Two of my three sons are into it. My eight-year-old is a specialist third man fielder — at both ends! He just makes up the numbers, but he loves it. While he probably doesn't really know why he wants to play, a lot of his mates do and some of his sporting heroes are top cricketers — guys like Ian Botham and Allan Border.

He makes a commitment to play every Saturday and is up with the birds, donning his whites, polishing some Kiwi into his sandshoes and rehearsing his shots. He meets his mates and off they go to a game, tossing by 8.20 a.m. and playing by 8.30 a.m., a time when most of us are still looking for a little shuteye.

On return, I'm all questions: 'Did you get a hit?' I ask. 'No, we lost only seven wickets, but we won.' 'Did you get a bowl?' 'Yeah, I had the last over and I got a wicket.' You can see the spark of excitement in his eyes. No problem with this bloke, you think to yourself. He's going to love the game all his life.

Cricketers young and old gain great self-confidence from doing something numerically positive against their names. And it's even better if their team wins. Cricket promotes lasting loyalties, friendships and dreams.

"THE TEAM TOOK THE FIELD!"

At one of my coaching clinics in Launceston, the boys listened attentively all day, practised their skills and went to bed in a high state of excitement. For on the morrow, they were going to play a match!

I remember two of the youngsters waking up in the middle of the night. It must have been 2 or 3 a.m. They were already dressed in their whites. They'd been dreaming of representing Australia. I asked them what were they doing and the kids replied earnestly: 'We 'aven't missed the game, 'ave we, Mr Walker? We 'aven't missed the game?' Their eyes were shining and their hearts were pumping. Talk about eat a cricket ball. These kids would have, too, if I'd asked them!

I remember feeling similar excitement at school before we played a match. These kids were just the same. At 10 they had the burning desire and ambition to compete. In time they could develop the obsession — and skill — which all great players share.

I don't know how the cricket bug bites or why a youngster suddenly downs all else — including his homework for next day's maths test, the TV guide or his skateboard — in favour of a little more bat 'n' ball practice. It just happens and in Australia we have more than 500,000 registered players, not to mention the kids who play on the beach, in the backyard or out the back of the local cricket oval.

Cricket becomes a love affair, far more complicated and intense than just playing the game, or adding up your runs and wickets. It's something which comes from within. A little kid picks up a bat, swings it once or twice, and wants to play. He might still be in three-cornered pants but he's having a go. I think that's tremendous.

Start 'em young, and make sure their bat is the right size — even if it means getting a saw and cutting off a bit! This young man, Christopher Magilton from Melbourne, favours an open stance with his hands nice and high on the handle. His cap could fit a bit better, but he looks keen enough and that's what counts.

Cricket — once bitten you're an addict for life. You'll play anywhere and if the beach is deserted, so much the better!

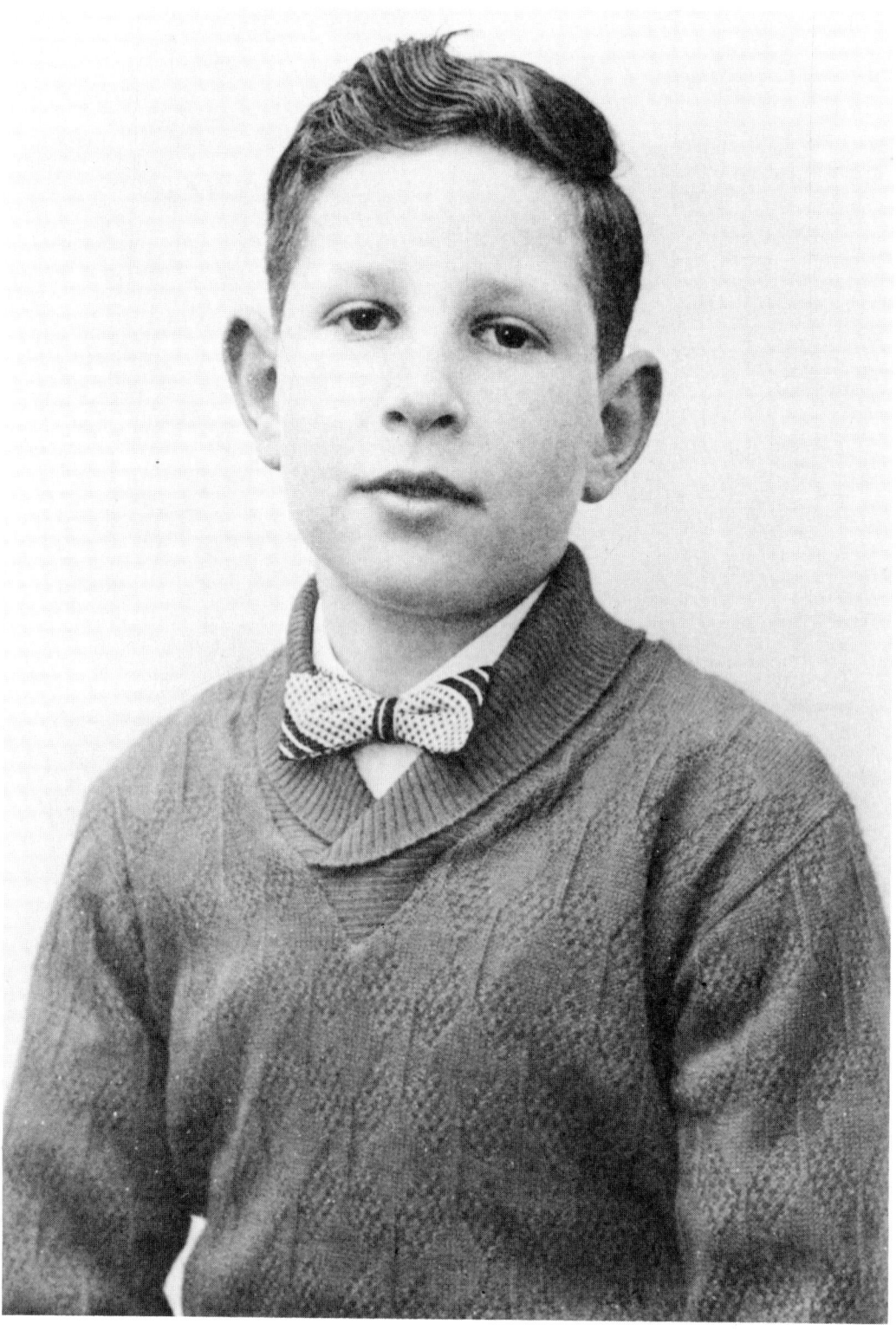

Yours truly, aged seven.

Batting

Bowling

Fielding

'A.B.' takes a wrong turn; Crocodile Dougie bites 'Chappelli'

EVERY CRICKETER has had an embarrassing moment. A couple I particularly like retelling both concern Australian captains, including current Test skipper, Allan Border.

'A.B.' had just been dismissed in a Test against England in Perth in the early 1980s and he stamped into the dressing rooms, very unhappy with himself for getting out, cursing England and 'bloody Pommie cricketers' in general. He threw his bat and gloves down and suddenly realised he'd taken a wrong turning and was *in the English dressing room!*

With everyone staring at him, Border went down on his hands and knees, picked up his bat and gloves, apologised to the England manager and bounded out the door to the 'safety' of his own rooms!

At least 'A.B.' found the right rooms this time... Flashback to the '84 Caribbean tour when Border and Terry Alderman (in the centre) helped Australia to a thrilling draw in the second Test in Trinidad. Border batted for more than 10 hours in this match and didn't offer a chance. He made 98 not out and 100 not out. The jubilant players are, from left, Rodney Hogg (front), Steve Smith, Tom Hogan, Carl Rackemann (obscured), Dean Jones, Kepler Wessels (obscured), David Hookes (behind Alderman), Roger Woolley, Greg Ritchie (behind Border), Geoff Dymock (assistant manager), John Maguire, Geoff Lawson and Kim Hughes (captain).

MY OLD mate and prankster Dougie Walters was at the centre of the next, an escapade involving skipper Ian Chappell during the '73 tour of the Caribbean.

Doug had laid his hands on a crocodile skin, a dreadful, slimy thing three feet long, which he proceeded to stuff, sew and adorn with two marbles for eyes. He called it 'Inshan'.

Dougie had been trying to hook 'Chappelli' for years and after some success in scaring his room mate Terry Jenner out of his wits, Doug went to work on Chappell.

The players had a day off from cricket and were going to play golf. Chappell had a favourite pair of diabolically loud red and white striped golfing trousers which he carefully draped over a chair in readiness before coming to breakfast in his shorts.

Dougie saw his chance, ducked into Chappell's room and slipped the stuffed crocodile into the crutch of Chappell's favourite trousers! Chappell came upstairs to change and, responding to Dougie's 'C'mon Chappelli, hurry up', quickly slipped into the trousers, only to come in contact with 'Inshan'.

Chappell screamed, jumped about, ripped out the crutch of his beloved golfing tweeds and fell to the floor entangled in a mass of shredded material and dead crocodile. Dougie couldn't believe his success. He was convulsed with laughter and even Chappell's stern vow to repay him didn't quell his mirth!

Australian XI players to head English first-class averages

Batting

YEAR	NAME	M	IN	NO	RUNS	HS	AVE	100s
1909	W. Bardsley	33	49	4	2072	219	46.04	6
1930	D. G. Bradman	27	36	6	2960	334	98.66	10
1934	D. G. Bradman	22	27	3	2020	304	84.16	7
1938	D. G. Bradman	20	26	5	2429	278	115.66	13
1945	K. R. Miller[†]	7	13	3	725	185	72.50	3
1948	D. G. Bradman	23	31	4	2428	187	89.92	11
1953	W. A. Johnston	16	17	16	102	28*	102.00	—
1956	K. D. Mackay	20	28	7	1103	163*	52.52	3
1961	W. M. Lawry	23	39	6	2019	165	61.18	9

[†] Australian Services XI
* Not out

Bowling

YEAR	NAME	M	O	M	R	W	AVE
1880	F. R. Spofforth	5	207	74	336	40	8.40
1896	T. R. McKibbin	22	647	198	1441	101	14.26
1934	W. J. O'Reilly	19	870	320	1858	109	17.04
1948	W. A. Johnston	21	850	279	1675	102	16.42

BCDEFGHIJKLMNOPQRSTUVWXYZ

Before you eat that orange…

RICHIE BENAUD, one of the greatest spin bowlers of them all, would bowl his leggies up to four hours a day when he was trying to make the Australian side — and longer when he actually got there.

Benaud believed there was no substitute for hard work. He developed a 'flipper', which tended to be faster and skidded into the pads of the right-handers, often catching them in front for lbw appeals.

At school, Richie would insist on an orange being packed in his lunch and before eating it, would flick it as hard as he could 100 times, like it was a cricket ball. He'd remain in the nets when others had long gone, or were out on the golf course. He'd get a box of practice balls and place a handkerchief on a good length, in line with the off stump, and see how many times he could hit it. He would bowl for hour after hour — no wonder he took 248 Test wickets, breaking Clarrie Grimmett's prewar record for the most Test wickets by an Australian

Instead of using an orange (or an apple), the medium-pacers should practise bowling a tennis ball — make it swerve in the air, this way and that, just as they'd bowl an in-swinger or out-swinger in a game.

Richie Benaud: 'The harder you work, the luckier you get.' He'd bowl for hour after hour in the nets; his batting was also world class.

Be in control at all times

POSSESSING A good temperament is important and being in control of your thoughts and actions is vital. However, if you're being slapped around by a batsman who is playing with abnormal luck, it's very difficult to maintain a sunny expression, especially if you are the one on the receiving end!

Master batsmen like Ian and Greg Chappell used to enjoy inciting fast bowlers. Viv Richards at his top was the same. He loved to get the new-ball bowlers 'in' and often succeeded, as Lenny Pascoe can well testify.

Viv used to say 'C'mon man' and bang, he'd strike another four. He arrogantly dismissed Lenny for three fours in a row at Adelaide in 1979-80. Big Len was furious and the madder he got, the looser his bowling became. According to the cricketers' 'bible', *Wisden*, Viv hit 13 fours on his way to 76 off just 72 balls. Len went for an average of six an over, finishing with 1 for 90!

I never had the pace to get involved in such head-to-head confrontations. Instead, I favoured a little 'reverse psychology' and would attempt to smile, even if I beat the edge or was hit for four. The smile generally became a huge grin on dismissing someone, but at least I tried!

Possessing the 'right' temperament is something you're born with, but it is possible to marshall winning feelings within yourself. Your match preparation should start early in the week, days before a game. Your pre-match aim must be to hone the forces inside you to a razor's edge. It's a matter of getting the blowflies inside your stomach into a straight line.

It's amazing to watch athletes or cricketers before they play a game. Some are tired and lethargic — the nervous energy has already exhausted them. A few jog up and down and can't keep themselves still.

Others like a Dougie Walters are completely relaxed. All Doug would want to do is have a cup of tea, a smoke and play a few rounds of cards.

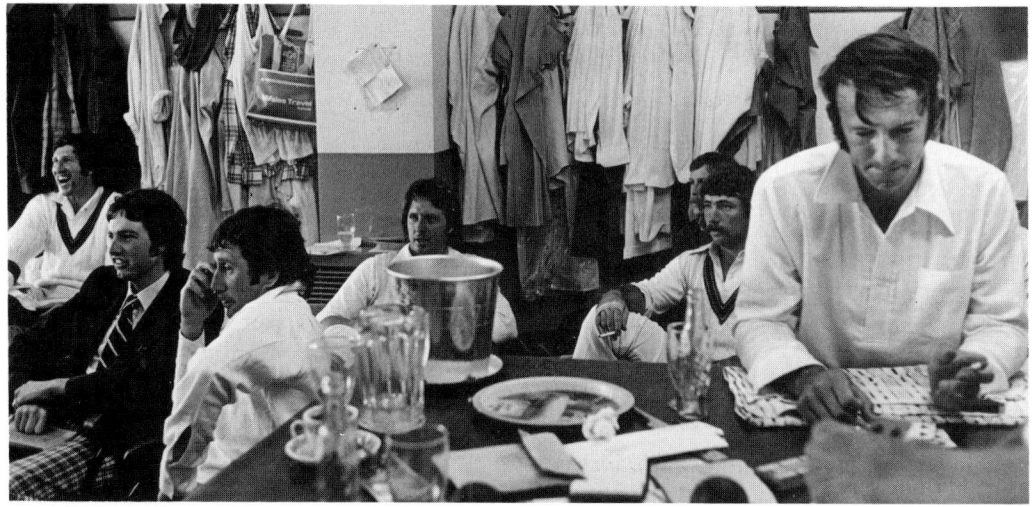

A pack of cards would never be far away when that great prankster Dougie Walters was about. If he couldn't get anyone to play with him, he'd deal to himself! His teammates, from left, are: yours truly, Ian Chappell (with Ashley Woodcock in 'civvies'), 'Thommo', 'Stumpy' Laird (obscured) and 'Bacchus' Marsh.

Dennis Lillee was totally in charge and knew exactly where he was at. You saw him gradually change his manner from his jovial entry, where he'd slammed the door and shared in a joke, to closer to the game where he practised with a purpose and become more and more introverted as he built himself up for the battle ahead.

By the time Dennis was last out of the pavilion — a personal superstition which mostly saw him straggle out at the end of the line — he was stern and already anticipating the challenge.

He'd bowled the opening overs in his mind. He knew what to do; he'd 'programmed' his mind to bowl certain deliveries to certain batsmen. Then, it became just a matter of carrying out the commands.

Even in the unforgettable Centenary Test revival week that we enjoyed as part of Australia's Bicentennial year, Dennis was the same…well, almost the same. As teammate Rodney Marsh said: 'Considering the night you had Dennis, the day was fairly useful!'

Eleven years after the actual event, we still had pride in our performances. When the National Anthem was played in front of 20,000 people before the first game in Perth, I thought to myself: 'This is unreal.' My old heart was pumping; it was like being 25 again and going out to face the world's best at Test level. When I got the first wicket, Bobby Woolmer caught behind, it was an incredible thrill and I jumped around like a wild man! I didn't worry about hiding my feelings then. A wicket is a wicket, even if it was a 'friendly'.

I'm told the best poker-faced cricketers included Herbert Sutcliffe, the great Yorkshireman; Australian skipper Herbie 'Horseshoe' Collins; and legendary Victorian batsman Bill Ponsford, who was utterly inscrutable.

'Ponny' loved batting. And batting. And batting. He remains the only man in cricket history ever to score two quadruple centuries. Not even Don Bradman did that. After making 352 for Victoria against the 'old enemy', NSW, in the mid-1920s, Ponny played a ball onto his wicket: 'By cripes I'm unlucky!' he said.

Ponsford had a favourite, baggy, blue Victorian cap. When he got to 100 it would be at a 45-degree angle and when he got to 200 — which was often the case — it'd be pulled down even further, with the peak splayed towards his left ear. You could tell the time of day and how many Ponny had scored just by looking at the position of his cap.

Bill Ponsford kept his emotions to himself and that must have been terribly frustrating to bowlers, looking for a glimmer of hope, or an acknowledgement that they'd just sent down a good ball.

Batsmen who are open and animated, who frequently show their emotions, are easy to 'read'. They're like an open book. If they keep to themselves, rarely having eyeball contact with the bowler, the better it often is. They are focusing on every ball and refusing to allow outside influences to interrupt their concentration.

Bowlers love to establish a psychological advantage. Lillee was a master at it. He would deliberately extend his run-through and finish eye-to-eye, giving the batsman his most intimidatory 'daggers' stare. I lost count of the batsmen who were obviously unnerved and soon forfeited their wickets.

I'm not recommending these tactics, incidentally, but they were an integral part of Dennis's philosophy. Successful fast bowlers must possess fire in the belly and there hasn't been a finer fast bowler in the game's history. 'FOT' — or 'Flippin' Ol'

Tart' — must have been doing something right!

In the current Australian team, Steve Waugh's expressionless disposition has earned him the nickname of 'The Iceman'. He's proved to be particularly valuable in crucial one-day situations, where he has few all-round peers. We are yet to see his best at Test level, but once he breaks through with his batting and scores the century we know he's capable of, he'll advance quickly at the five-day game, too.

In my own career, I'd never snared five wickets in an innings until I took 6 for 15 in my second Test against Pakistan at the SCG.

When it did come, I thought to myself: 'Hey, why not every game?' It was as simple as that. Steve Waugh has found it difficult as so many people talk about his inability to go on and make a Test century. It has probably created a mental block.

Out in the middle, Steve appears very composed and relaxed but inside the butterflies are probably rampant. It's just that he puts a lid on his emotions. That's the way he is and in time he'll become a great cricketer.

Steve Waugh, 'The Iceman' of Australian cricket, plays professionally 12 months a year, with NSW and Australia in our summer and in English county ranks with Somerset during winter.

'C'mon Tangles, think about it. You can get this bloke — just put it here, and make him do that.' I go through a little mental rehearsal while walking back to the bowling mark during the summer of 1974-75.

Bottoms up!

THE 1977 tour of England was just looking up, too. Although we'd lost the one-day internationals, were behind in the Tests, and the formation of World Series Cricket was making front-page headlines everywhere, a few of us, especially the Victorian element, were starting to come good.

Richie Robinson had made 70 not out and 137 not out at Warwickshire and in the final warm-up before the third Test, I took 7 for 45 against Leicestershire.

We went to Nottinghamshire confident of squaring the series. An Australian Test team hadn't been beaten there since 1930 and even the comeback of the redoubtable Yorkshireman Geoff Boycott or the debut game of a likely, young, Somerset buck, Ian Botham, didn't overly concern us.

We met the Queen late on the first day — Dennis Lillee wasn't there this time to say 'G'day' — and even our first innings score of 243, although lowish, could have been far worse as we had been 8 for 155.

Lenny Pascoe and 'Thommo' opened the bowling and broke through several times, giving us the start we needed. I was down at fine leg and got the nod from the skip to warm up. I'd already done a few windmills and hamstring stretches in preparation for a bowl and wasn't particularly perturbed when a few members of my fine-leg 'fan club' started yelling: 'Nice bum, Tangles. Do you always wear that colour of knickers?' and things like that.

I wasn't going to acknowledge them. After all, it was the second day of the Test, a Saturday holiday, and the people had paid their money and were entitled to have a good time. I just walked in a bit and then walked backwards, refusing to even look at them. I continued to limber up, touching my toes again. This time they all started whistling. Even a couple of girls joined in. 'Bacchus' Marsh and the blokes in slips turned around to see what was going on, but I couldn't tell them anything.

About the fourth ball of the over, I walked in and nervously touched the back of my pants and realised what the commotion was about — there was no cloth covering my bum! The stitching had ripped from the belt line right down to the bottom of the trousers. To double my embarrassment, I had one of those old, football-type jock straps on, which expose the cheeks of the bottom. Here I was, flashing my derriere to all and sundry!

I couldn't get off quickly enough to find a new pair of strides and I was still beetroot red when I emerged a few minutes later, safely decked out in a substitute pair.

I was telling Bobby Willis and Tony Greig about this one night and they had similar tales — though not quite as revealing as mine. Bobby, as captain of England, was walking out to bat after a break and forgot to bring his bat with him!

He walked down the pavilion steps and onto the ground, checking to make sure he had everything. He went through his routine: pads, gloves, protector, thigh pad and then it dawned on him — he'd left his blade behind!

A few years earlier, during the memorable 1974-75 series, 'Greigy' was marking guard against a hyped-up Dennis Lillee at Brisbane when he realised he had forgotten his protector. Dennis — in his comeback Test — was pawing at the ground off his long run-up and Greigy knew he'd be 'for it' after bouncing out Dennis in our innings. But he decided that as there were just a couple of deliveries to go to the end of the over, he'd tough it out and call for a box at the change of ends.

Dennis charged in and the first one climbed past Greig's throat at a most alarming rate. 'I didn't need any prompting then,' said our forgetful star. 'I just walked off and left Dennis standing there. There was no way I'd face another ball without one, with him in *that* mood.'

Bradman and the greats

SIR DONALD Bradman once said that when you stop learning the game of cricket, it's time to get out. He was aged 75 at the time and still considered himself a student of the game. For more than 30 years after his retirement as the greatest player the cricket world has seen, Bradman served as a selector and as an administrator. He turned 80 in 1988 and still takes a terrific interest in the game.

Bradman's enthusiasm for cricket took him to Sydney, via the Bowral train each Saturday morning. He'd be up before dawn and wouldn't get home until midnight. It was a very long and arduous day but he did it every week, for several years, before shifting to the city and making his name.

Bradman hadn't played a lot of turf cricket but learnt and adapted his game as he gained more experience. He learnt lessons from the good — and the bad players — just by watching and taking it all in. He evaluated the strengths and weaknesses of his opponents and became one of Australia's greatest captains.

His playing record is incredible and probably will never be surpassed. His feats are extraordinary. Legend has it that a young, outback cricket fan listening in the wee hours of the morning via crystal radio to Bradman hitting the Pommies all over the ground in far-off England, said: 'Cripes if he's doing that when it's dark, how many would he make in daylight!'

Here is Sir Donald's playing record for Test, first-class and minor grade cricket:

Test career

	Tests	Inns	NO	Runs	HS	Ave	100s	50s	Ct
1928-29 v England	4	8	1	468	123	66.85	2	2	2
1930 v England	5	7	0	974	334	139.14	4	0	2
1930-31 v West Indies	5	6	0	447	223	74.50	2	0	4
1931-32 v South Africa	5	5	1	806	299*	201.50	4	0	2
1932-33 v England	4	8	1	396	103*	56.57	1	3	3
1934 v England	5	8	0	758	304	94.75	2	1	1
1936-37 v England	5	9	0	810	270	90.00	3	1	7
1938 v England	4	6	2	434	144*	108.50	3	1	0
1946-47 v England	5	8	1	680	234	97.14	2	3	3
1947-48 v India	5	6	2	715	201	178.75	4	1	6
1948 v England	5	9	2	508	173*	72.57	2	1	2
Totals	**52**	**80**	**10**	**6996**	**334**	**99.94**	**29**	**13**	**32**

Summary

	Tests	Inns	NO	Runs	HS	Ave	100s	50s	Ct
In Australia	33	50	6	4322	299*	98.22	18	10	27
In England	19	30	4	2674	334	102.84	11	3	5
Totals	**52**	**80**	**10**	**6996**	**334**	**99.94**	**29**	**13**	**32**

Career batting record in all cricket, first-class and minor:

	Inns	NO	Runs	HS	Ave	100s
First-class cricket	338	43	28,067	452*	95.14	117
Minor cricket	331	64	22,664	320*	84.88	94
Totals	**669**	**107**	**50,731**	**452***	**90.26**	**211**

* Not out

C DEFGHIJKLMNOPQRSTUVWXYZ

Can little Johnny ring home? His mother is worried

I WAS just thinking to myself how successful day one of my very first coaching clinic at Assumption College, Kilmore, had been when a police car roared up and two officers stepped out.

'You're Max Walker aren't you?' said one.

'Yes,' I said.

'Is this your coaching clinic?'

'Yes.'

'Do you have a kid here called Johnny so-and-so.'

'I guess so,' I said. 'There are 269 of them here. Take your pick!'

The policemen said little Johnny hadn't been in contact with home since his mother left him at the school the day before and she was worried! I explained to the officers that there weren't too many telephones around, the kid was probably having a good time, and most likely hadn't given a thought to ringing home.

The mother must have given the policemen a real grilling. 'But he's never been away from home for 24 hours or more,' the boys-in-blue continued. 'Can Johnny please get in touch with home?' I nodded, said I'd do my best and off they went.

The camps are designed for the kids to have fun and relate to one another, as well as learn the game's fundamentals. We don't encourage the boys to ring Mum on the hour. There's no need. They are so engrossed. Their fascination and enthusiasm to learn the game helps to bind them together. The four days are over in no time.

Some of the kids who attend the camps have never been away from Mum before. They are able to share their experiences — eating, training, crying and hurting together. They watch pictures and have lots of fun. That's the way it should be.

If they remember two or three things about cricket at the end of the day, that's terrific. We don't saturate their minds with technique. It's a fun thing. I'm gratified that some of the kids swap addresses and correspond. The only time they ever see each other is each year at the camp.

My idea of successful coaching isn't to be a 'stand-over' man. I won't 'over-coach'. If the child is making runs or taking wickets, it's not for me to stamp my value judgement on him and change him all around. He's doing more right than he's doing wrong.

Why alter a child's natural style? He may be a budding Dougie Walters or Jamie Siddons, an uninhibited shot-maker who would only become frustrated having to conform. I say, let the kids hit the ball as hard and as long as they like.

One of the greatest cricketers of them all, West Indian Sir Garfield Sobers, never used to have his foot that close to the ball when he caressed it through the covers. But he was poetry in motion. Kiwi Lance Cairns hit the ball as far as anyone I've ever seen. Six sixes in 10 balls at the MCG in a one-day match against the

Aggressive Victorian batsman Jamie Siddons stepped into international ranks in September 1988 when Australia toured Pakistan. He's one of the brightest young talents in the game.

Lance Cairns, one of the great hurricane hitters of the game. His bat weighed 3 pounds 10 ounces; it was enormous. This shot from the Kiwi all-rounder has soared into the grandstand, judging by 'keeper Bobby Taylor's gaze.

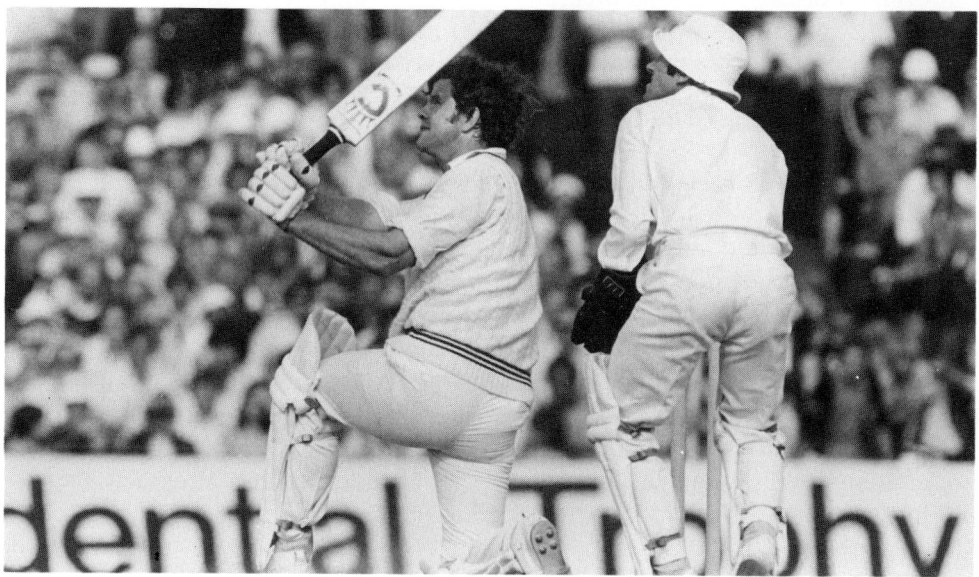

Australians was an amazing exhibition of hitting.

When my cricket skills were forming, there were few coaching manuals to consult and they were couched in language I couldn't understand. Ever seen anyone bowl right-arm over left earhole with his legs crossed?!

Caught on a sticky

1. From a batsman's point of view

BATTING PROVIDES particular challenges when the wicket is wet and 'popping'. If the sun shines, often the turf will become 'gluey' or sticky and many of batting's normal practices must be ignored.

An aggressive outlook is essential and with close catchers often stacked around both sides of the wicket, lofting the ball is also often essential.

Bowlers can be unplayable so it's necessary for a batsman to try and dictate terms. Consider batting out of your crease to upset a bowler's length. Don't go just six inches, go a good two feet down the wicket, taking care to note the position of the wicket-keeper, to avoid being stumped in case you miss the ball.

You're highly unlikely to be bowled out or lbw in these conditions. Being caught is the only logical way. The ball will pop, but very slowly, making strokeplay difficult unless the ball is pitched right up, or short.

Make the bowler come to you, allowing his good balls to pass over the top of the wicket and going after the ones just a little over-pitched or short of a good length. By playing your shots, you'll soon scatter the close-in fielders, lessening the opportunity of dollying an easy catch. Suddenly the bowler and the wicket will not appear quite as dangerous.

It's hard work batting in these conditions. You have to be patient and wait for the loose ball. If a delivery is short of a good length, it's unlikely to hit the wicket, even if it pitches on the stumps, so let it go. A bowler will soon become exasperated seeing the ball climb over the top all the time. He'll try something different and this is where a batsmen can capitalise on looser deliveries.

2. From a bowler's point of view

MANY BOWLERS feel that wickets will come automatically or without too much thought once a wicket is sticky, the bounce awkward and defensive play dangerous. But line and length bowling is even more of a factor in these situations. If you're loose, the good batsmen can really benefit.

Bowlers must keep the ball up, on a good length. If you bowl short, you're in for a hiding, especially against quality batsmen.

Fielding positions and strategies also become important. Sometimes a deep backward point or a short third man are handy for the skied attempted drive. You have to 'read' your batsmen, work out those who will try and take the attack to you and those who are more likely to block and balloon a catch. Having the same field for two totally different batsmen is poor planning and poor cricket.

Colour cricket — via the radio

THE OLD Tasmanian Cricket Association (TCA) ground in Hobart was never the warmest place to be and no matter the weather forecast, we'd always pack some soup in a thermos, along with sangers, a bat and ball, scorebook and portable radio. No one had invented ghetto blasters then!

When the rains came, it was a desolate place, especially if you hadn't seen a touring team for three or four years and now were being denied that privilege by Mother Nature!

The only consolation was tuning into the radio boys and listening to all sorts of cricket banter, as they tried to fill-in time during the interruptions.

In those days, Tasmania wasn't a full-time member of the Sheffield Shield competition and the big cricketers came to Hobart or Launceston only occasion-

John Arlott: incredible knowledge, humour and presentation.

ally, usually when international teams stepped off the mainland between New Year Tests. As I understand it, we only got to see the West Indies on their 1951-52 tour because the Calypso skipper John Goddard wanted to see friends on the Apple Isle!

The closest we'd get to Test cricket in those days was through the eyes of master commentators John Arlott, Alan McGilvray and Charles Fortune. They'd light fires inside us, even when it rained, with their incredible knowledge, humour and presentation.

I lost count of the times I overslept and missed getting to school on time after having stayed up listening to the ball-by-ball description of a Test from England. John Arlott's prose were always a delight and even for English county games, I'd make sure I tuned in at 7.30 a.m. each day for McGilvray's touring reports. Later, I was to have the pleasure of working with 'Mac' and other cricketing legends.

Relating the on-field pictures I saw into homes around the country — and giving people pleasure in the translation — became a joy for me in my time with the ABC before joining Channel Nine and attacking fresh challenges.

Copycats
(or, how to improve yourself by watching others)

CRICKET IS such an intricate sport that you could have several lifetimes and still not know it all. Trying to learn from your own experiences as well as by watching others is some of the best advice I was given back in my teen years. Not only did I find the best players provided the lessons, so too did the not-so-greats, through their mistakes.

When the Test cricketers come to town, youngsters should try to get to a day's play early — when the players are limbering up — and absorb the lessons. They'll notice the points particular batsmen and bowlers are working on. They'll see how hard the slips fielders concentrate and how easily they pluck the ball out of the air.

From the current Australian team, the top four batsmen, skipper Allan Border, openers David Boon and Geoff Marsh and No. 3 Dean Jones, each have different skills.

Hooked on Cricket

Former international Shaun Graf clutches a flyer from Greg Shipperd, Victoria versus Western Australia, December 1981. Johnny Scholes (first slip) backs up.

Slips catching practice with the Victorians at the Junction Oval, from left: Dean Jones, Tony Dodemaide, Ian Frazer, Jamie Siddons and Dav Whatmore. Notice how Whatmore, a master slips fielder, has bent his knees, to help take low ones.

Resolution could be Allan Border's middle name. When he grits his teeth, few bowlers can get the ball past him. He's pictured fending one towards square leg, on his way to 62 not out in the dramatic Christmas Test against England in Melbourne in 1982-82. Bobby 'Chat' Taylor is the 'keeper and Geoff Miller the slipsman. Border, partnered by my old mate Jeff Thomson, added 70 for the last wicket before Thommo was caught with Australia just four runs short of what would have been a remarkable victory.

Dean Jones shows beautiful balance and footwork during the third Test, Australia versus England at the Adelaide Oval, December 1986. The midwicket fielder is England's Allan Lamb.

Few hit as hard as Victorian and Australian all-rounder Simon O'Donnell. Bowling against him in the indoor nets can be positively dangerous!

I never cease to marvel at Border's application and determination. Sometimes he displays an almost arrogant attitude towards bowlers, believing — quite correctly — that he is their superior.

Boon is a fine strokemaker, but he's also tightened his game defensively, the result of hour upon hour in the nets. I thought he was always going to have trouble with the one that leaves him — the short of a length delivery which jags away to the slips— but he worked very hard, disciplined himself not to follow the moving ball and had a career-best season in 1987-88, his performances surpassing even those of Australia's batting supremo, Border.

After making his 100 at the 'Gabba against New Zealand, Boon said he thought the best shots of his innings were the ones he didn't play — the deliveries he allowed through to the 'keeper. He became far more selective. He worked out whether he should go forward or back, decided to let the dangerous ones go, and go after only those to his liking.

At Test level, deciding which stroke to play has to be an instantaneous decision, especially against new-ball bowlers. There's a lot to debate in just a few hundredths of a second. The good batsmen appear to have extra time in which to play their strokes. They strike the ball late and always appear classy, in-control types.

Dean Jones is one of our most exciting strokemakers, although sometimes too impetuous for his own good. He's very quick between wickets — probably the fastest in the current Australian team — and while he occasionally 'turns blind' in his keenness to turn two into three, he's working hard to fine-tune his skills.

Greg Chappell used to be the classic role model for youngsters. Now one of the most technically-correct players is Simon O'Donnell, a free-flowing striker of the ball who has the ability to bat higher than No. 6 or 7.

Youngsters wishing to emulate the stars should watch their heroes closely, working out which are their favourite shots and exactly how they play them. That'll provide the basis — the rest is up to you.

Day of the doodlebug
(or, the fastest ball I ever faced)

WHEN YOU'RE six foot three inches and 14 stone in the old measurements, you don't tend to scare too easily, but I'll never forget the doodlebug Michael Holding sent down at me at the Sydney Showgrounds during World Series Cricket.

I was caressing the ball nicely and was into my 20s when Michael really let one go. Usually you have some idea where the ball will pitch, but I completely lost track of this one until it was beside my nose. At that stage my composure deserted me. My legs went from under me and I lay on the ground like a huge, vibrating starfish.

The gold Kookaburra whizzed past my face and bounced about a foot in front of West Indian 'keeper Deryck Murray. In my daze, I can recall this big, dark shadow looming over me and saying: 'Sorry Muxie, Sorry Muxie.' I didn't have a helmet on and in a split-second, my whole life had passed me by. I can't remember what I said to Mike — for one of the few moments in my career I was speechless!

I've only ever been 'beaned' twice and both times Michael Holding was my tormentor. However, I've got a lot of respect for Big Mikey (who hasn't!). I believe the first doodle he delivered was a dead-set, honest mistake, but I'm not sure about the second.

'Big Mikey' Holding of the West Indies, the Rolls-Royce of fast bowlers.

'Sorry, skip, I can't control my feet!' — Derek Underwood on facing Michael Holding during the '76 series in England.

It was at Jamaica during one of the first one-dayers of our '79 tour. 'Thommo' and I were the last blokes to bat and we still needed a dozen to win. I must have been irritating them, banging that big front foot of mine down the wicket and playing forward to virtually everything.

The light was fading when big Michael let one go which I didn't even see. I felt it whoosh past my nose at about 100 mph and wondered if winning a silly old cricket international was really all that important!

Thommo, at the safety of the non-striker's end, broke into a giant grin, no doubt thanking his lucky stars he hadn't been on strike. I eventually managed to scuttle to his end and somehow between us we stayed there, got the dozen runs for victory and ran off like two big kids who had stolen two ice creams.

We won only two of the one-dayers in that series and played almost a dozen games so that win was pretty good value. But I still have nightmares about that ball — no wonder they called Michael Holding 'Whispering Death'!

Doing the quickstep

MY SPORTS master at Friends' School — Noel Ruddock — had some novel practice innovations. At the start of a session, he'd get us to bat with a stump, throw the fast bowlers a brand new cherry, and say: 'Let 'em rip!'

Some of the boys were quite lively, especially on the school tracks. You'd have to really concentrate, move your feet quickly and watch the ball like a hawk. After 10 minutes, Noel would say: 'Change!' and we'd reach for our favourite bats and suddenly be playing enormous shots with the confidence of a Richards or Border.

Another one of his innovations, aimed at stopping a player from 'lifting' his back foot — or backing away — was to tie a piece of rope around the batsman's foot and stake it to the stumps! I still laugh at that one. An alternative he used was for a guy to hang onto the batsman's back foot while another threw the ball, but that proved a bit risky if the bowler strayed down the leg side!

The one I favour to encourage players staying in line against faster bowling is to position a brand new cricket bat, face up, against the striker's heels and make sure he's wearing sprigs! Obviously the player won't step back for fear of damaging the bat — especially if it's his own!

I've always kept my cricket theory simple, mirroring the thoughts of my Dad, Big Max, who advocated all-out attack and hitting the ball as hard as it was humanly possible. He reckoned that when you found yourself down the track after advancing to a slow bowler, you might as well play a shot rather than block.

That philosophy got me into a lot of trouble over the years. When I should have been plonking a dead bat on them, I was trying to dob them over long-on for six. Sometimes it worked, sometimes it didn't, but they could never say I wasn't entertaining!

EFGHIJKLMNOPQRSTUVWXYZ

Excuse me Mister, can I have your autograph?

AS A youngster, and depending which end of the wicket I stood, I'd imagine I was Normie O'Neill or Ian Redpath, playing shot after shot against the world's best. If I happened to have the ball, there was no argument— I was Wes Hall.

I'll never forget the first time I saw the great West Indian bowl. It was at the old TCA ground in Hobart and he was pushing off the sightscreen. It was a most intimidating sight. He was bowling to an in-form Bobby Simpson who struck four or five

One of my childhood idols: Wes Hall, aged 19, arrives in England for the 1957 tour. Hall was fast and furious, a tremendous athlete.

fours in a row. I was awestruck as Wes would reply with an even quicker — and shorter — delivery. He bowled terribly fast. It really made the blood race. I thought: 'This is it. I'm going to be a fast bowler.'

I clutched my autograph book tightly and looked at the clock to see when the next interval was. I had to get closer to this man. I wanted to see if he really was seven foot tall! Above all, I wanted his autograph.

Officials were manning the dressing room and keeping the kids right back. We had no chance going through the front door. The back door was locked but there was a louvred window for the toilet...

Quick as a flash, my mate had bunked me up and I was pulling out all the louvre blades from the window. I shimmied my way up and I was in.

I came down with a crash and entered the dressing room, which was old and antiquated with hardly any light. All I could see was the whites of their eyes and their teeth. One said: 'Hey man, what you doing in here?' I mumbled something about wanting to meet Wes Hall and thrust out my autograph book. The great man himself signed it and I got nine or ten others of the magnificent 1960-61 team as well.

Lance Gibbs, Sir Garfield Sobers, Cammie Smith, Conrad Hunte — they are names forever etched in my memory. As a very impressionable kid, I thought I was in heaven. I said to myself: 'I have to be like these guys.'

I'd discovered the joys of autograph-hunting and as I got older, I remembered the kindness of the West Indians and always tried to accommodate the youngsters who wanted my autograph.

Unfortunately, not all Australian players have followed suit. I was shocked when walking out of the rooms with a couple of better-known fast bowlers at the Melbourne Cricket Ground during the mid-1970s. A young boy ran past with a bunch of clippings he wanted autographed. It was obvious he didn't want mine.

Sign please, mister... Australian fast bowler Craig McDermott looks slightly daunted by a long line of autograph hunters at Assumption College, Kilmore, in 1985. The line of enthusiastic young cricketers got even bigger, too! Talk about popular...

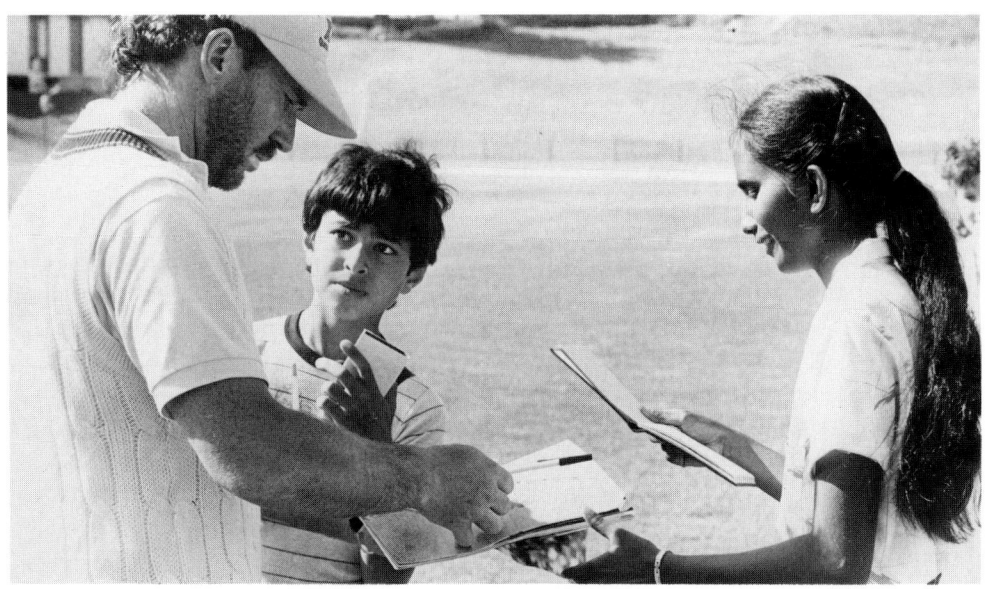

Australian skipper Allan Border pleases a couple of young fans in Sydney. Some cricketers find signing autographs a chore but for me, meeting and chatting with fans is what it's all about.

One of the cricketers said: 'Nick off kid, I'm in a hurry!' You could see the tears well up in the youngster's eyes. His role model, as far as the boy was concerned, had been destroyed. It's a scar he probably still carries today.

The player should have said: 'I'm sorry, young fellow. I'm flat chat. Come back tomorrow and I'll sign one for you, your mate and five or six others, too.' Unfortunately he didn't.

I thought to myself: 'What's so special about you? You're luckier than most in that you're able to play Test cricket. But you had the opportunity to play. That kid is just as important. Given half a chance he might be up there, too.' The fast bowlers strolled on, uncaring, leaving the kid to his unsigned clippings.

The high profile cricketers have a huge burden to carry. They are busy but they should never forget their beginnings — when they were that age and collecting autographs. The youngsters today are fanatical about the game, just as we were. They can tell you Allan Border's Test and one-day batting average, where he was born, everything. They can reel off the same detail about Ian Botham and Richard Hadlee or any of the stars.

I was very statistically minded, too. I could recite just about every number of every guy playing in the Tasmanian Football League and all their facts and figures.

The kids who enjoy the cricket the most are the ones who dream a lot, get their scorebooks and sit there with their thermos and rugs. They score every run and plan and plot like they were on the field, representing their country. They put themselves in the captain's shoes — 'yes, I would have done that', or 'no, that was a bad mistake'. Cricket is a way of life.

I sat through many a physics class at Friends', rolling my pencil, complete with all its etchings — one, two, three, four, no ball and wicket. Every now and again there'd be a 'Howzat!' and everyone would look at me. But I was oblivious — Wes Hall had struck again.

Fancy a bowl?

THE BACKYARD at the Empire Hotel was long and narrow and as the patrons streamed out the back on the way to the boys' room, I'd tap them on the shoulder, with bat and ball in hand, and casually say: 'D'ya think you can get me out?'

I was quite small and skinny in those days, and the blokes would laugh, roll up their sleeves and think I'd be easy to knock over. But all that practice at school must have been doing me good, as I generally played them all right. If they overpitched, I'd try and hit it back as hard as I could.

There wasn't much value in shots square of the wicket. The slash over point often meant a broken kitchen window, while a hook shot only went a few yards, straight into the side fence. The most satisfying shot was the straight drive, with which I could get 'value' even if the best-hit shots endangered the guest bowlers who sometimes were hit on the shins or on the knee and were forced to 'retire' inside for a reliever!

My sister, Lexie, almost two years younger than me, was one of the best bowlers. She had a nice side-on action, too, nothing like mine!

Depending on the season, we'd play footy or cricket. The backyard was our domain and the Test matches or kick-to-kick competitions were fiercely contested.

With all the practice I was having — at school and in the backyard of the pub — I soon graduated into the North Hobart senior XI. It caused a bit of a stir as I was only in middle school and was all of 13 years old!

Actually I was lucky to get a game. A guy dropped out at the last moment and I was thrown in. My highest score was only 29 in the seconds, but somehow I managed 66 not out in the firsts and was on my way.

It was a battling knock and none too elegant. I was continually being hit on the pads by the leg spinner. Instead of the ball spinning away from me, it kept ducking back all the time. It was quite mystifying. My partner down the other end, Tony Hill — who taught me mathematics at school — explained that the leggie was bowling 'wrong 'uns' and I should be very watchful.

Tony was a terrific fellow and I thank him for getting me through matriculation maths with a few credits — as well as on that afternoon, helping to unfathom the wily leg spinner's 'shock ball'. Again it was cricket which had founded — and cemented — the friendship.

Fine tuning your skills

* Saving a split second in the field

THIS IS a good one for cricketers of all ages and can result in a valuable run-out or vital runs being saved: When chasing the ball in the outfield, many players are inclined to pick the ball up on their right-hand side, wheel around, take a step and then throw the ball back to the 'keeper. If they happen to be more than 40 or 50 metres away from the wicket, alert batsmen invariably can sneak another run.

However, by picking the ball up on the left-hand side, and off the back foot, you're already side-on and your feet are positioned to throw almost in the one motion.

A split second is saved by this positioning of the fielder's body and by not having to wheel around to throw. Batsmen who may have been contemplating a third run will stop, go back and be wary of your ability from then on. Suddenly, you're in a position to save up to 10 runs in every innings.

* *When catching*
KEEP YOUR fingers 'soft', the hands cupped with fingers pointing skywards, if the ball comes to you above the belt buckle, or fingers pointing down for anything below the waist.

* *When running between wickets*
DON'T TURN 'blind'. Always know what the fielder is doing, especially when you want to take that extra run on his arm. If you know he can throw and he's in the 'mid-distance' throwing area, about 50 metres from the wicket, turn and go back. Don't risk it.

There are only three calls — yes, no and wait. The striker calls when the ball is in front of the wicket and the non-striker when it's hit behind point or behind square leg. The crease is the cut-off point.

Don't let anyone call *all* the shots. You owe it yourself not to get run out. When

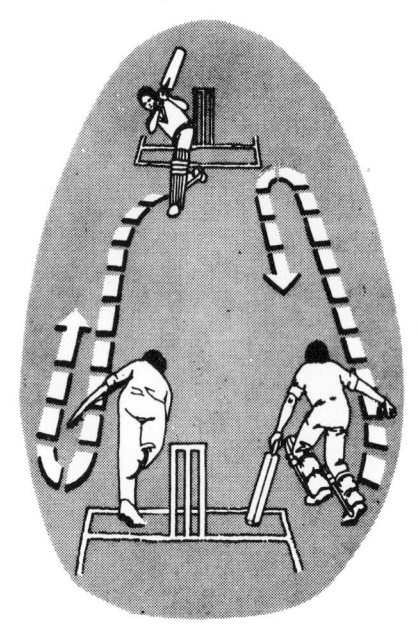

When running between the wickets, stick to opposite sides of the pitch. The striker usually runs on the same side from which the bowler has delivered. The non-striker takes the opposite side, avoiding any chance of collision.

Bowling close to the stumps at the popping crease has enormous advantages but it's difficult to break bad habits unless there are 'obstacles' in the way of your normal path, as practised by Mike Whitney in the New Year of 1988.

you're calling, you control your own destiny. When it comes to the crunch — and the heat of a run-out — only a few will sacrifice their own wicket to allow you to continue batting.

* Play one ball at a time

EVEN in schoolboy or club cricket, bowlers can sometimes produce a delivery which would do justice to the Test arena. It might swing late in the air, cut off the wicket, bounce wickedly or spin at a virtual right angle.

With any luck, it might do 'too much' and miss the edge of the bat or the stumps.

Don't be daunted. You can receive only one delivery at a time. If you see off the one which has really seamed or spun, the odds are with you. Sooner or later, you're going to get a delivery of lesser quality — one which allows you to score a run and scuttle up to the 'safety' of the other end.

Bobby Simpson and Bill Lawry, our greatest opening pair before the Boon-Marsh combine, would alternate the strike cleverly. 'I was always trying to get to the other end,' Lawry would say. 'It was safer up there!'

* Keep your eye on the ball

IT SOUNDS simple but even the greats sometimes err. You *must* watch the ball in the bowler's hand, not just the 'general image' of the bowler coming in to bowl.

When Australian batting great Greg Chappell again started focusing his attention on the ball in the bowler's hand after a bad run of 'outs' early in the 1980s, he immediately regained his touch.

Even the best players have times where they don't know from where their next run is coming. So, when you're 'in' and seeing the ball well, take advantage of it.

Rain interrupts play? It doesn't mean an end to competition, as shown by South Australian Shield players Rod McCurdy (left) and David Hookes, at the MCG in December 1984.

Always be on the look-out, however, for the ball which could defeat you. Over-confidence invariably leads to premature dismissal.

* Adapting from matting to turf

YOUNGSTERS INVARIABLY learn the rudiments of the game on concrete wickets covered with matting, malthoid or artificial grass.

On mats, the ball tends to bounce more and lead to more back-foot play, and when youngsters progress to turf ranks, they take time to adapt to the lower bounce.

On turf, players must develop front-foot play so as to reduce the deviation from the track or the risk of being caught in front of the stumps by one which skids through low.

Good mat players often struggle at first on turf. They get caught in 'no man's land', neither forward nor back. That's when they must practise even harder and get a mate to throw the ball at them from a short distance so they can get the feet moving again.

When I first started in Tasmania, we'd play on concrete wickets with the old composition balls. I was lucky — we graduated to turf at Friends' School and having all that practice as a teenager stood me in good stead later on.

* The power of planning

PREPARE YOURSELF mid-week for a weekend game; make some notes about it. What are your aims? What is the likely condition of the ground and the wicket?

If you're a bowler, mentally prepare yourself to bowl 20 to 25 overs. Actually visualise yourself bowling a tight line and length. If you're a batsman, be prepared to bat for three or four hours, survive the early part and be the backbone of the team innings.

By the Friday night, you should have already played the game in your mind — and won, making runs or taking wickets yourself. Come match day, there's no self-doubt when you walk through the gate. You've been there before. You know you're going to succeed.

At the Los Angeles Olympics in 1984, one of Australia's four gold medallists was weightlifter Dean Lukin. His was a gutsy effort, considering that his major opposition, an American, had lifted two kilograms more than Lukin had ever lifted in his life. But Lukin had dreamed of being a gold medallist. This was his chance. He focused his thinking positively.

You've seen the weightlifters prepare for a lift: they stand motionless, sucking in the air. They shut their eyes, actually visualising themselves competing. They can feel the bar, the texture, the chrome plate and the resin on their hands. Their thighs burn, their legs vibrate and they pick it up.

This was Lukin's moment of truth. He could be champion of the world or he could run second. The crowd start singing 'Waltzing Matilda'. Lukin hardly hears them. He's concentrating on what he's going to do. He wants the gold. He's confident he can do it. All this happens in a matter of seconds. In his mind, Lukin has made the lift, the biggest of his life. He opens his eyes. Suddenly it's the real thing. Seconds previously he's made the lift. Why not do it for real?

Super heavyweight Dean Lukin: during training, he'd shut his eyes and imagine he was actually making a successful lift. Having done it in his mind, he found the actual lift easy.

He starts the actual lift with the crowd roaring encouragement. He can't hear them. With one gigantic heave, he gets the bar above his head, stands still and throws it jubilantly to the floor. He's done it; he's won the gold medal. He prepared himself to win gold and he's done it. By thinking positively and rehearsing the lift, Lukin brought glory to himself and his country. The best golfers like Greg Norman and company also visualise their shots, where they will land and how close to the pin.

Winning cricketers can also prepare themselves for a successful weekend. It doesn't matter if they are aged 10, 20 or 50. I tell my son Tristan to go to bed and play shots. He takes a cricket bat with him and I'm sure he's already made a few centuries at the MCG!

* *The benefits of footwork*

DEAN JONES is one of Australia's most enterprising batsmen; he hits the ball hard and once set, is very hard to restrict. In this photo series, Jones takes the attack to the bowling, firstly with an off-drive against a slow bowler and secondly, with one of his square cuts against a faster bowler.

His footwork is excellent in both photographs — his head remains still, his eyes focus completely on the ball, while his feet take him into the best position to play the shot. His feet are quite wide at address but he feels comfortable that way, even though it may not be classic MCC coaching manual material.

Youngsters wanting to emulate the stars do not need to rigidly follow their hero's every movement or mannerism, but rather adapt their game to what suits them best.

This five-photo sequence shows Dean Jones executing a dancing drive (used against slower bowlers).

...And here is the Dean Jones cut (to a fast-medium bowler).

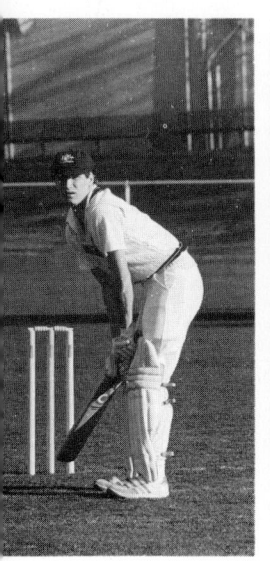

Got problems? Hit them head on!

PRACTISE EXACTLY as you play. Perfect practice doesn't make you perfect, but it will make you a whole lot better. If you're slip-shod at practice, you won't advance on match days. Cricketers needs to be motivated and enthusiastic. When cricket becomes a chore, that's when you get out.

People say to me: 'Maxie, don't you ever get tired with all this cricket, cricket, cricket? You played and now you commentate. Doesn't it bore you?' Dull minds may find it dull and boring; I don't.

Youngsters should always be working at ways to improve. If they play good length bowling well, but struggle against anything a little shorter, they should practise coping with this weakness until it's a strength.

If they don't like bouncers, there's nothing like getting a string of short ones to help overcome that fear. Conversely, if a youngster doesn't drive well, he should have someone throwing the ball from 10 metres, work on his footwork and gain confidence as he starts to hit them in the middle.

None of my captains asked me often to field in the slips — they must have preferred to have me running the boundaries, using my natural pace! But that didn't stop me from becoming involved in slips catching practice. It's good for your reflexes and when you start grabbing a few, it's great for your self-esteem.

The only way to overcome problems is to hit them head on.

Happy snaps

CRICKET PHOTOGRAPHY has been a fascination of mine ever since my Dad showed me how to use our old box Brownie. What started as a bit of spare-time fun has now become a most expensive hobby, as it must if an enthusiast's whim is to advance.

I started with a small Canon, which I bought from legendary Sydney photographer Ron McKenzie during the '73 tour of the Caribbean, and gradually updated from there. Now I have a Minolta 7000 with all the whizz-bang gadgetry. I was unofficial team photographer during our World Series Cricket Caribbean tour in 1978-79 and have been click-clicking away happily ever since. I've collected some beauties along the way and here's a selection:

Photography has always been a fascinating hobby for me. I was the unofficial team photographer when we toured the West Indies with World Series Cricket in the late 1970s.

> *Centenary Test, 1977. Cricket immortal Clarrie Grimmett, then 86, meets my big Springbok buddy, Tony Greig, who somehow had talked himself into being captain of England. Both have a beer in their hands. Clarrie was introduced to the amber nectar by another great slow bowler, Bill 'Tiger' O'Reilly. 'He remained eternally grateful, too,' said Bill.*

Tony Greig again, on the beach in Sydney in 1976 with his daughter Samantha. Trust Greigy to bring a brand-new bat down to the water for beach cricket. He endorsed St Peter bats in those days and was on such a big whack that he could probably afford it!

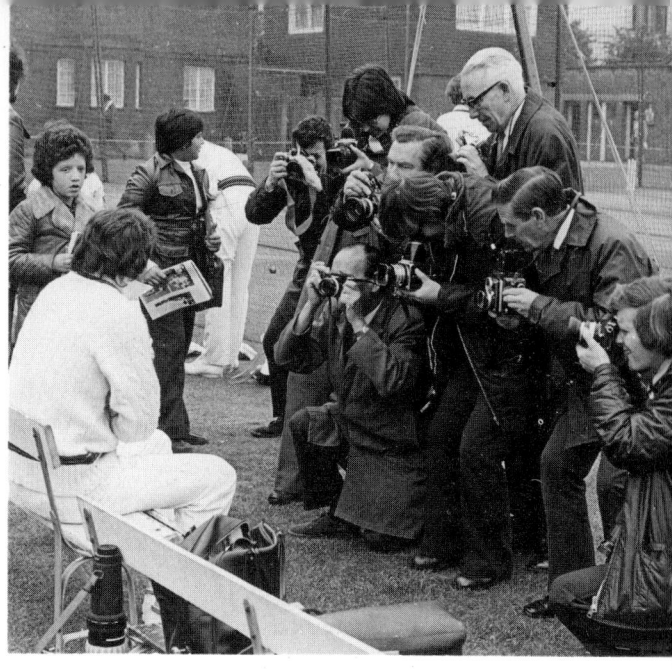

So this is what it's like to captain Australia: Ian Chappell at Lord's in 1975. Eight cameramen went for the front-on head and shoulders shot; leading English cricket photographer Patrick Eagar (far right) found a different angle. Chappelli always worked in well with the media boys, realising the value of good public relations.

At least I didn't say 'G'day', like Dennis Lillee (pictured next to Dougie Walters on the far left). Perhaps Queen Elizabeth appreciated this as we discussed the hot weather and how to remove Friar's Balsam stains from dainty gloves! I was so keen to shake her hand during the tea interval at Lord's in 1975 that I forgot I had my bowling hand wrapped in Balsam and cottonwool and boy, did it make a mess! We did get on famously, however, and no one cared that the break went longer than usual.

Dennis Lillee said he was the hardest man in cricket to dislodge, so when I rolled plucky English left-hander John Edrich during the '75 Test tour, we were all pretty happy. Little 'Eddy' just loved batting and one day at Sydney occupied the crease for two and a half hours for 30-odd not out after earlier having two ribs broken by Lillee. The Sydney Hill crowd was unbelievable that day, chanting 'kill, kill, kill' as Lillee ran in to bowl. At the other end, Thommo bounced several lots of four byes over Rodney Marsh's head, much to Marshy's disgust.

He's still the best cricketer in the world, by a street: when the great Viv Richards turns it on, he adds a fresh dimension and excitement to the game. This shot, taken by Ray Titus during Australia's 1984 tour, heralds another Richards century, in front of his home crowd at Antigua. They treat him like a God there and in many ways, he is. Carl Rackemann is the long-suffering Australian trundler.

Lord's 1975: Would you believe that the rotten little cherry bounced on Derek Underwood's wicket but failed to knock the bail's off! I wasn't too impressed as I'd already bowled 20 overs for 'one-for' and, as you can see by my countenance, it was nice and hot out there. 'Deadly' Derek looks mesmerised and well he might have been —I'd given him the Maxie special, the one which wobbles a bit before cutting back late off the wicket. I thought it was far too good a delivery for Deadly and I still didn't get him out! Such is the lot of a bowler down on his luck.

Despite my much-discussed tangle-footed approach to the wicket, I can't recall ever bowling five no-balls in a row, a fate which befell West Indian quickie Joel Garner at Melbourne in the 1984-85 Christmas Test. Umpire Steve Randell, Tasmania's only representative in the Test match, called big Joel for overstepping six times in one over of the Australian first innings. The over lasted 12 balls — and 10 minutes — much to Joel's gigantic disgust.

How to get autographs when the teams are out of town

OFTEN THERE is a four-year gap between full-length tours of Australia by the most popular teams such as England and the West Indies. Obtaining team autographs can be difficult because of this.

The Australian team plays at the major capital cities throughout December and January, but if you live in the country, or don't have the opportunity of going to the cricket, gaining player autographs is also a problem.

But there are ways. The best is simply to write to the person, explain who you are, how old you are and why you want his autograph. Enclose a stamped, self-addressed envelope so all the player has to do is autograph the bit of paper or the enclosed photograph. Send it care of the player concerned, wherever the side is playing. The mail is sorted and distributed to touring cricketers each day. Allow two days in 'posting time' so a player gets it at the start or during a match.

If the game was in Melbourne, this is how I'd write my request letter:

22 December 1988 (insert the relevant date)
From: John Smith (insert your name)
26 Chappell St., (insert your address)
Prahran 3181 Victoria

To: Steve Waugh
c/- The Australian cricket team
Melbourne Cricket Ground
Yarra Park,
Jolimont 3002 Victoria

Dear Steve,

My name is John Smith and I am 10 years old. I have been following your career with a great deal of interest and like the way you are always involved in the game, especially in the one-day matches.

I enclose a newspaper clipping which includes the picture of you bowling Gordon Greenidge. Could you please autograph it for me?

I also enclose a piece of white cardboard which I'd like you to sign for my collection. I thank you very much for your time and I hope we can beat the Windies this Test match.

Yours sincerely

John (insert your name)

Here are the addresses you'll need, depending on where the players are based:

VICTORIA
c/- The Victorian Cricket Association
66 Jolimont St.,
Jolimont 3002
Victoria

NEW SOUTH WALES
c/- The New South Wales Cricket Association
47 York St
Sydney 2000
New South Wales

QUEENSLAND
c/- The Queensland Cricket Association
PO Box 197
Woollongabba 4102
Queensland

SOUTH AUSTRALIA
c/- The South Australian Cricket Association
Adelaide Oval
North Adelaide, 5006
South Australia

WESTERN AUSTRALIA
c/- The West Australian Cricket Association
WACA Ground
East Perth, 6000
Western Australia

TASMANIA
c/- The Tasmanian Cricket Council
PO Box 525
Rosney Park 7018
Tasmania

Don't forget: Address your letter to the player concerned, enclose a stamped, self-addressed envelope and allow a couple of days in posting time.

How to multiply your batting average by four

YOU KNOW you can play better. You're keen to improve. You've studied last season's stats and know you have one or two weaknesses. So, how do you prepare yourself to be a better cricketer?

You see the Test match when it comes to town, watch all the one-dayers, but when it comes to getting past 20 in your own Saturday afternoon competition, you invariably fail, ending up in the doghouse after taking out your frustrations on the wife's favourite cat.

The good players know what to do. They listen to their bodies and analyse their actions. They know what their limitations are and they play within a self-imposed set of rules. They practise and practise their strengths and come match day, play to their pluses. They succeed more times than not and the very best go on to represent Australia.

Ask any of the current Test team and they'll admit to having one or two 'do nots' for their own game. Geoff Marsh tries not to hook early in an innings. Fellow opener David Boon tells himself to ignore deliveries pitched just outside the off stump. Both wait until they are set before bringing in their best shots. It's a commonsense approach to batting and one we could all copy — no matter our stature.

Put it this way: if you go for a job interview, you don't march in and say you're good at two or three things but hopeless at anything else. You outline your strengths and hope that those skills are enough to get you the job! Cricketers should also ascertain their strengths and concentrate on them.

I spoke with the great West Indian wicket-keeper/batsman Gerry Alexander prior to the 1975-76 series in Australia. He told me how he used to have these magnificent dreams of being able to cover drive like Normie O'Neill, hook like Neil Harvey and square cut like Grahame Thomas, three of the most exciting postwar Australian strokemakers.

'I wanted to do it all,' he told me. 'I'd get great 16s and 18s but then get out. After one of these little knocks, someone whispered in my ear and said: "You know, you should forget about the cover drive. You don't hook well and you hit the ball in the air when cutting."

'I was told I should dump the three shots which really excited me. It was hard to do but the results were miraculous. By eliminating those shots, I started to make runs — regularly.

'I was a good off driver because I could keep the bat straight. I could work the

Geoff Marsh and David Boon are the best openers since Simpson and Lawry. They are pictured, with Kris Srikkanth, during their record-breaking 219-run stand, third Test v. India in Sydney, January 1986.

West Indian Gerry Alexander increased his batting average from 15 to 60, just by eliminating the shots which used to get him out.

ball for ones and twos through mid-wicket. I glanced well and could keep the ball out all right. So I built my whole game around those three aspects, all the time working on a tight defence. Suddenly, I became a key number in our batting line up.'

Alexander was averaging just 15 in 20 previous Tests, yet in 1960-61 he topped the West Indian batting averages, ahead of legendary batting trio Rohan Kanhai, Garfield Sobers and Frank Worrell, scoring a century in Sydney in the third Test on his way to making almost 500 runs for the series. His average? 60-plus. What a transformation!

I loved the big hit too much to drop it from my repertoire, but it just goes to show what a little discipline and commonsense can achieve.

If any cricketer goes back and analyses how he got out, 80 per cent of the time he'll find he was out hitting the ball in the air. That only comes from having too much bottom hand in the actual stroke. Unless you are defeated by a very good delivery which hits the edge, the only way to hit the ball in the air is to give it too much bottom hand.

Analyse everything and when in the middle, concentrate on your strengths. You can work on other parts of your game in the nets. Talk to as many people as possible. My chat with Gerry Alexander came too late to turn me into a specialist batsman, but I can relate to the remarkable turnaround in his career.

In recent times I've advised guys like Merv Hughes to get involved in as many of the after-match conversations as he can, especially if he finds himself sitting opposite some of the true greats such as a Richard Hadlee or a Dennis Lillee. Players can glean so much from chatting to the best. They not only enhance their friendships, they learn by listening.

Just before the World Championship of Cricket, the one-day international spectacular run in 1985 as part of Victoria's 150th year celebrations, I remember Richie Benaud was sought out by little Laxman Shivaramakrishnan, the Indian leg spinner, during a break in the commentary.

Indian leg spinner Laxman Shivaramakrishnan, a terrific talent and one who may not mature as a world-class bowler until his late 20s.

The first thing Richie said to the baby-faced youngster was: 'Do you really want to be a Test-class leg spinner?'

The young man's eyes twinkled. 'Yeah, yeah, I do, I do,' he said.

Richie repeated his question. 'No, do you *really* want to be one?'

The young man again said 'Yes'.

Richie then asked him why he hadn't come down to the nets to practice on the previous day. Little Shiva said: 'Well, it wasn't compulsory.' Richie explained how hard he'd worked at the same age. He told Shiva: 'You should have gone down there in the morning, in the afternoon, grabbed some kids and bowled to them and when they got sick of it, bowled some more. You should be the first down there and the last to leave. You must practise and then practise some more. In my prime I could run in with a blindfold on and pitch the ball on a good length.'

Richie looked at Shiva and asked: 'How old are you?'

'Nineteen,' came the reply.

'Well you've got about eight years before you're going to be even half reasonable! Do you still want to be a leg spinner?' The young man shuffled his feet. 'Don't be disheartened,' Richie cut in quickly, 'you've got to understand that this is what it's going to take for you to be totally in control.'

Australia's No. 1 fast bowler Craig McDermott was in for the same shock when Dennis Lillee outlined the workload necessary to become a consistent Test wicket-taker. Craig had arrived like a meteor and suddenly lost his way. He was really struggling by the time he sought out Lillee. Dennis said: 'I run five or six miles every day of my life. I push weights, do exercises for my back and upper body and after all that, I bowl and bowl.'

To his credit, McDermott has buckled down, works as hard as anyone in the Test team and, after some knee trouble, is re-establishing himself.

How to stop a 'steam train'

YOUR TEAM is 6 for 46. The pitch is popping. The bowlers have their tails up; it's a tough predicament. How do you stop the 'steam train?' If you let the situation get the better of you, wickets will continue to tumble at a runaway rate and your side will soon be all out.

The worst thing a batsman can do in this situation is to analyse too closely the previous dismissals. He can become overawed by the task he faces and start to believe that every delivery is virtually 'unplayable'.

Often, in his panic, he fails to realise that the special deliveries came when the ball was at its hardest and shiniest. He forgets there's a fair chance batting will be a little easier when he's in, even if his side is six for not-too-many.

It can be depressing to see the other lads come in. They throw down their bats and hang their heads. Morale is low and it can go shooting through everyone, even the guys who are yet to bat. If you walk into a conversation where the talk is all negative, it's hard not to be brought down to that level yourself. You have to walk away from it, remain positive and confident that you can succeed.

Watch champions like Allan Border walk in to bat. They'll invariably look up at the sun, blinking in the extra light, helping prepare themselves for the challenge

Down but definitely not out: Allan Border rarely loses his poise at the crease, or his footing, but ended up flat on his back in the Caribbean during the 1984 second Test in Trinidad, though still with his bat at the ready. Border's stalwart efforts against the West Indian fast bowling 'steam train' were one of the few highlights in a losing series for Australia.

ahead. The less time spent looking at the fieldsman or the bowler the better.

You keep your thoughts to yourself, take block and work hard at eliminating all possible risk. Try and play only the balls which are a danger to your wicket. Work at your defence. Think about the areas where the opposing captain and his bowler are trying to get you out.

As a bowler, you should be able to sum up their strategy fairly easily and be familiar with what the bowler is doing, if only through your casual around-the-ground stroll and careful study behind the bowler's arm earlier in the day.

Don't pre-judge or pre-select what's going to happen. Try to give your partner, who is probably one of the specialist batsmen, as much strike as possible.

If you can get by with six singles and you're in a partnership of 30 or 40 in a situation like that, those six singles are invaluable. You must have 'stickability' (Richie Benaud will frown as he doesn't reckon it's a word). Crease occupation becomes paramount. The run of quick wickets falling must be stopped. Don't worry about the scoreboard. Sure it's a serious situation but if you stay there, runs will come.

Even the good players are forced to grind if they come to the crease at 2 for 0 or something similar. No matter how dazzling their reputation is for strokeplay, they are going to be on the back foot and forced to defend for quite a long period, until the immediate danger passes. It's easier for the specialists than for the batting 'bunnies', thereby adding to the challenge.

'Deadly' Derek Underwood acted as England's nightwatchman for most of the 1974-75 series. The going was torrid, particularly for a No. 9 batsman. He often found himself coming in to bat when the second new ball had been taken.

Ian Chappell would have ensured that his two main strike bowlers, Dennis Lillee and Jeff Thomson, had been rested and capable of bowling flat out right from the outset. Having to face them at full tilt was quite a proposition for a recognised batsman, let alone a tailender.

38 Hooked on Cricket

England's 'Deadly' Derek Underwood obviously is not enjoying this fast one from Dennis Lillee, Centenary Test, Melbourne, 1977.

Veteran Colin Cowdrey of England is struck on the forearm by Jeff Thomson in Perth during the 1974-75 season. Thommo was lethal in this series, bowling as consistently fast as anyone in the game.

I can still picture Derek's courageous efforts to keep the ball out of his stumps and away from his body. His feet would splay in a most ungainly pose and with eyes bulging like light globes, he'd ward off the ball. It was an unenviable and frightening position.

Cricketers, especially those at Test level, are expected to handle the heat, but when they lack the ability of others, it's easier said than done. Deadly took an enormous psychological battering.

Left-handed Englishman David Lloyd was shell-shocked by the Thomson–Lillee attack.

After that pace-dominated Australian series, the West Indies toured in one of the next English seasons (1976) and Michael Holding, the 'Rolls-Royce' of speedsters, really made his name. He bowled very, very fast. Deadly again found himself batting against the second new ball and after his Australian experiences, he found it physically and psychologically very difficult.

In one Test, before Holding had even let another lethal delivery rip, Deadly came running at him. He was four paces down the track with the bat up around his ears, trying to hit the West Indian speedster out of the ground.

He did it three times in a row, and failed to connect three times. His batting partner, England skipper Tony Greig, came down the wicket and said: 'Stick in, stick in.' Deadly replied: 'Sorry Greigy, I don't know what it is, but I've got absolutely no control over my legs or my body or anything!' The scars of facing Lillee and Thomson at their quickest had re-opened.

Another Englishman, left-hander David Lloyd, also had tough times against the two speedsters and in Perth was hit with such force in the groin that his protector split in half. I swear he turned green! It's something he'd still have nightmares about.

Happily for us all, genuine fast bowlers, especially those who hunt in pairs, are not a common commodity in cricket. When the time comes, however, it's a matter of overcoming the tendency to jump away — force yourself to hang in there. Otherwise 6 for 46 will quickly become 7 for 46 and that 'steam train' will soon tear through the whole line-up!

'I'm going to England to play cricket, not sign #$ä%@ autographs!'

AS AN Australian team going to England, we were expected to have 7000 team sheets autographed before we got off the plane in the 28 hours between Sydney and Heathrow.

Each pad contained 50 sheets and a few of the more scholarly types, like 'Thommo' were far from impressed. He'd curse: 'I'm going to England to play cricket, not sign #$%@ autographs!' However, he still signed, even if it was just a scrawly 'J.T.' and was voted by the rest of us as the worst autograph ever.

My Victorian teammate, Richie Robinson, on his first big tour, started his task full of vim and vigour, his sleeves rolled up and spare pens at the ready. He started the first pad carefully putting circles over his i's, but in the end he was plain 'R. Robinson', an obvious sign of fatigue!

Still, our efforts would have been worthwhile. The kids in England are really into autographs and most of the 7000 sheets would have gone off in the first month.

Later, we learnt that the great Australian batsman Sidney Barnes had procured a rubber stamp of his signature, an investment we all thought would have been money well spent after all our labours. If only we'd known…

With the Compliments of
20th Australian Team to Great Britain 1948

Bradman, D. G. (Captain) (South Australia)	*[signature]*
Hassett, A. L. (Vice Captain) (Victoria)	*[signature]*
Barnes, S. G. (New South Wales)	*[signature: Sidney Barnes]*
Brown, W. A. (Queensland)	*[signature]*
Hamence, R. (South Australia)	*[signature]*
Harvey, R. N. (Victoria)	*[signature: Neil Harvey]*
Johnson, I. W. (Victoria)	*[signature]*
Johnston, W. A. (Victoria)	*[signature]*
Lindwall, R. R. (New South Wales)	*[signature]*
Loxton, S. (Victoria)	*[signature: Sam Loxton]*
McCool, C. L. (Queensland)	*[signature: John McCool]*
Miller, K. R. (New South Wales)	*[signature]*
Morris, A. R. (New South Wales)	*[signature]*
Ring, D. (Victoria)	*[signature]*
Saggers, R. (New South Wales)	*[signature]*
Tallon, D. (Queensland)	*[signature]*
Toshack, E. R. H. (New South Wales)	*[signature]*
Johnson, K. O. E. (Manager) (New South Wales)	*[signature: Keith Johnson]*

Sid Barnes, one of Australia's greatest cricket characters, had a rubber stamp made of his signature (highlighted above) and paid a youngster five pounds to stamp the hours away while the 1948 team was on the boat to England. The young man's aim was not always what it should have been! (Autograph sheet courtesy David Frith.)

'Johnny Won't Hit Today' and other great one-liners

I'VE SCRIBBLED down many humorous crowd comments over the years, both from my own experiences and from chatting to cricket fans around Australia and beyond.

I'll never forget the guy in the Caribbean who offered me his wife as a 'reward' for taking the wicket of Lawrence Rowe during the 1972-73 tour!

'Hey Wocka, hey Wocka,' he yelled. 'You bowl beaut ball. See that gal over there. Thars my wife. She yours. She yours.'

I looked across and spied this big fat mama grinning at me. When I say big, I mean BIG! She and her mates all had the giggles. I reckon she would have been ideal in a back pocket at the MCG; someone to prop up the goal post with. You wouldn't get anything past her, such was her width.

I tried to be polite as possible in turning down his offer, but my new mate went on unabashed.

During the next over he asked me: 'Okay, Wocka, if you won't take my wife, whaddabout a drink? Whaddabout a drink? Are you hot, are you hot?'

Hot! It was a good 45 degrees out there and he thrust into my hand this great bottle of rum and invited me to to take a swig.

Coke, lemonade, even a beer would have been right up my alley but a bottle of 300 per cent proof rum which had been sitting in the sun all day was something else. In the interests of multinational goodwill, I pretended to take a swig, much to the delight of the immediate crowd who'd taken a lot of interest in my vocal mate's conversation.

We've had some great and witty barrackers in my time but I'm sorry I missed the most legendary, Sydney rabbito Stephen Harold 'Yabba' Gascoigne, who was renowned for his humour on the SCG Hill during the 1920s and 1930s.

He once suggested to a bowler who was continually beating the edge of the bat: 'Send 'im down a grand piano, mate, and see if he can play that.'

To less successful bowlers he'd say: 'Yer length is lousy but ya bowl a good width.' When a batsman who had struggled to get off the mark finally squeezed a single, Yabba commented: 'Whoa there, he's bolted!'

Popular Englishmen Maurice Tate and 'Patsy' Hendren were great favourites of the Hillites, Patsy for his antics which included ceremonious bows and curtseys when he had thrown the ball in over the stumps and Tate for his big feet, which were often the centre of attention. Yabba reckoned Tate was forever retying his shoelaces. When he bent down to do up his shoelaces for the umpteenth time that day, Yabba said: 'Thank goodness he's not a flamin' centipede.'

When an umpire held his hand aloft for some time waiting for the attendant to move the sightscreen, Yabba commented: 'It's no use, umpire, you'll have to wait till playtime like the rest of us.'

When Jack Hobbs played his last match in Sydney, the members of the Hill

Sydney's 'King of the Hill', Stephen Harold 'Yabba' Gascoigne, the legendary cricket barracker of the 1920s and '30s.

chipped in and bought him a present, an ornate boomerang. When Hobbs walked around to the Hill to receive his gift he asked for Yabba and shook hands with him.

I can't imagine any of the present-day champions walking around to Bay 13 to do that, but I used to love them all and will never forget the tumultuous reception they gave me over after over during my personal best Test performance, 8 for 143 from 42.2 overs against the Poms in the final Test of 1974-75.

I've lost count of the people who have walked up to me and said they were in Bay 13 that day, but it was an enormous crowd and they really looked after me that afternoon.

I've got quite a collection of favourite one-liners. Here are a few of the more printable: Former England captain Johnny Douglas had the initials J.W.H.T. and the Aussies dubbed him 'Johnny Won't Hit Today'. During one of his particularly slow innings, a barracker pleaded: 'Fetch a cop someone and pinch him for loitering.'

In one MCG game, Douglas was batting during the last hour of play and to amuse themselves, the crowd took bets on how many trains would come past the Jolimont end of the ground versus how many runs Douglas would score in the same period. The trains won 17 to three! Another Englishman, Trevor 'Barnacle' Bailey, was even slower. One day at Sydney someone yelled: 'Why don't you drop dead Bailey?' A mate followed: 'Whaddayamean, he is dead!'

In 1974-75 when 41-year-old Colin Cowdrey was flown in to help bolster the English batting, he batted courageously in Perth against the fire of Dennis Lillee and Jeff Thomson. As one whistled past his ear, one wit yelled: 'That's the spirit, Thommo, rattle out a tune on his false teeth.'

The first time perky Derek Randall batted in Australia after his Centenary Test triumph was in an up-country game at the start of the 1978-79 MCC tour. He studiously played a maiden over, whereupon a wag in the crowd yelled: 'Aw, c'mon Randall, you wouldn't get a kick out of an electric chair.'

All good, humorous stuff. No one took offence and that's the way it should be.

Kanga Cricket — it's fun but...

FOR THE uninitiated, Kanga Cricket is terrific. You have a short hit or a couple of overs with a plastic bat and ball and most of Australia's primary schools now play it.

However, I'm not a great advocate of the game, especially when four or five of the group may already be quite proficient, yet have to hang around waiting for another chance. Some might get bored. Some might slide back a level and become frustrated as their advancement isn't as immediate as they'd hoped.

What we must do is become more preoccupied with excellence. It has to start in the classroom, with the teachers who help frame the 'local' rules.

Why should they make kids retire at 25 in some of the games? If the lad is good enough, why can't he go on and get 75 or 100? He might nick three or four through the slips, steer a couple of twos and suddenly he's 25 and being asked to come off. He might be just starting to find his feet, realising he's good enough to amass a big score. Fellow Channel 9 commentator Tony Greig told me that by age 10 he'd already scored 10 centuries at school. The South African system allowed it; ours should too.

Some say that one or two youngsters who open the batting might dominate every week and not let anyone else into the game. Okay, let the No. 10 and No. 11 guys open in the next game, it'll soon sort them out. If a boy is good enough, he'll show it. But they shouldn't be penalised or asked to stop batting just because they're good.

Bill Lawry, a former Australian Test captain and great opening batsman, would bat through his lunchtimes at Preston Technical School. Legend has it that he once batted for five weeks in a row. Even the teachers couldn't get him out! The great turn-of-the-century batsman Victor Trumper went one better and stayed in for *six weeks* at the Crown Street School in Sydney when aged 10 in the 1880s.

Youngsters should be allowed to play as well as they can, make a level and strive for the next one. From 13 and 14 years of age, the very best lads are just three and four years away from playing Sheffield Shield cricket, and on the verge of Test cricket selection.

Look at Dougie Walters: he was 17 when he made a half-century on debut for New South Wales and 19 when he emulated the legendary Bill Ponsford's 40-year-old feat of hitting centuries in his first two Test matches. Current Test pair Steve Waugh and Craig McDermott were also teenage prodigies, coming into the highest ranks very early.

If a lad wants to play the game badly enough, nothing should bar his way. Young kids dream of batting for Australia. Unless they can really 'feel' the cap on their head, it's probably not going to happen. When Dav Whatmore first played for Australia, he was so proud of his baggy green cap that he'd wear it around the house, even when doing the washing!

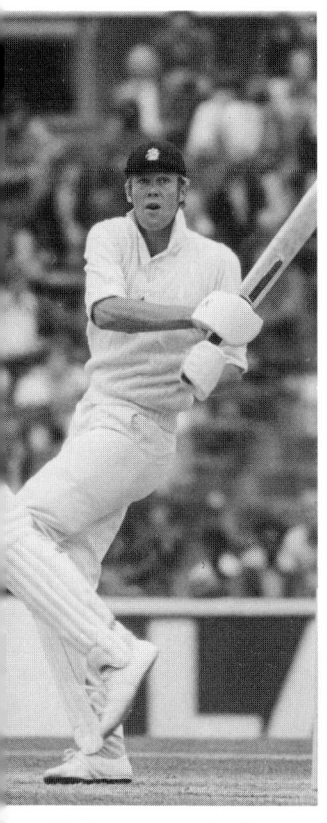

Tony Greig: 10 centuries in school cricket before he was 10 years old.

Bill Lawry: even the teachers at Preston Tech. couldn't get him out.

At 19, Doug Walters made successive tons in his first two Tests.

Lads can hope, but there's a big difference between hoping and desperately wanting something. To succeed you have to be totally obsessive. You've got to eat, drink, sleep and talk cricket. A lot of parents aren't going to like that, as there are many setbacks along the way. It takes an incredible amount of time and hard work to mature into a top liner.

Elite players can 'read' which way the ball is going to swing, not only by just watching it out of the bowler's hand, but by gauging the body action of his opponent. That doesn't come from just reading a book, or talking to a great player. It comes from doing it, as often as you can, for hour after hour, until your mates or your Mum refuse to bowl any longer!

Legends and how they start

WHILE I'M just a touch too young to have seen him bat, I've read how Don Bradman was renowned for starting an innings with a tuck for one to backward square.

Greg Chappell loved to stand up very elegantly and classically ping his starting delivery just wide of mid-wicket. If you kept pitching on leg stump, he'd continue to hit you through the mid-wicket gaps and would be into his 20s and 'away' before you realised it.

Dougie Walters had an unusually fine square drive which often rattled the pickets at forward point. David Hookes, South African legend Graeme Pollock, and West Indian Sir Garfield Sobers, three renowned postwar left-handers, also possessed this shot. They seemed to do it naturally but few right-handers could do it with Dougie's results.

When he scored his 250 at Christchurch, New Zealand, in 1976-77, he hit the ball through square with such ferocity that he had the blokes at point and cover lifting their hands and giving it the 'green light' on the way through to the

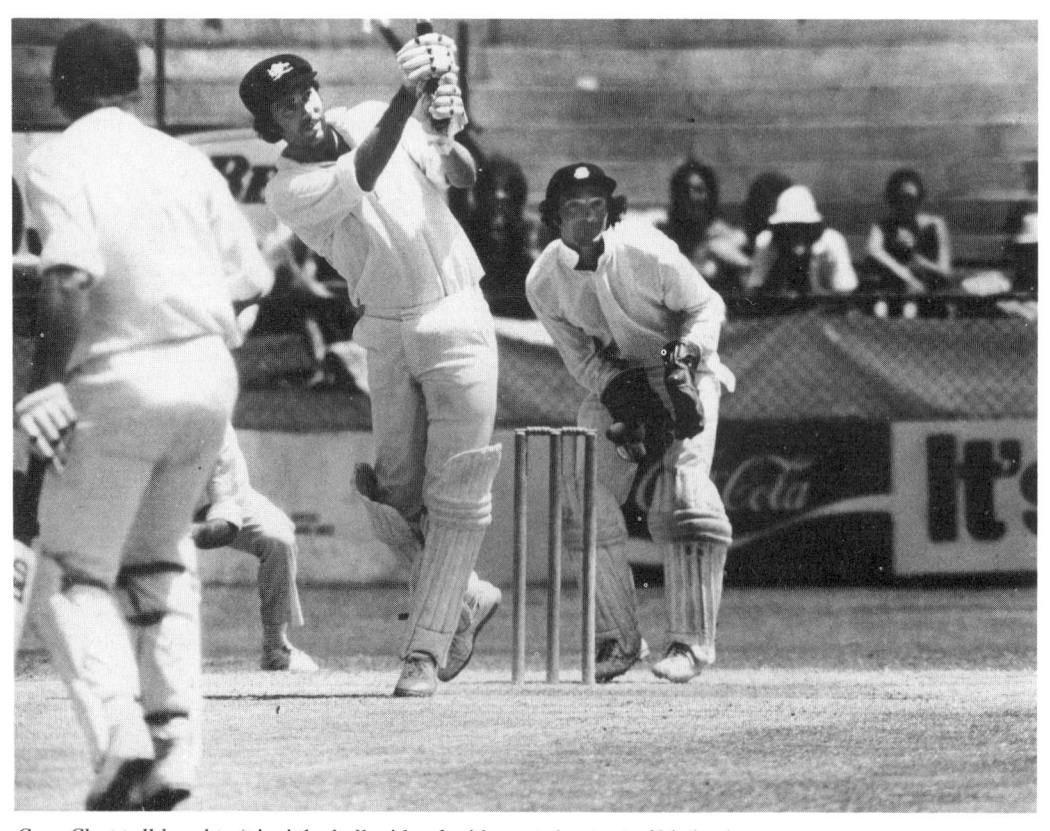

Greg Chappell loved to 'ping' the ball wide of mid-on at the start of his innings.

'If you're going to get that far down the track, Maxie, there's no point blocking.' I remembered those words of wisdom from my father throughout my career. Here I am opening the shoulders in a charity game in Darwin. It was so hot that day that taking the long handle was always going to be my plan. Notice the high follow-through — eat your heart out, Greg Norman!

boundary. They weren't interested in stopping them at all. Dougie hit the ball really hard that day.

He could get into trouble on the back foot with that defensive shot of his which saw the bat come through on a 45-degree angle, but when he was on the front foot, he was a very difficult player to bowl against.

Ian Chappell was a good hooker but he also loved to hit the ball straight down the ground. He was one of the first to use a heavier bat. He and brother Greg made the Chappell 'V' famous. Early in an innings, they'd do away with virtually any shot other than a drive between mid-off and mid-on.

Allan Border's favourite is a flat-bat pull, a real baseball shot, which sees him tug the spinners from outside the off stump way over mid-wicket. It's very effective.

My personal preference was to go for the 'big one' over mid-on. My Dad would say to me: 'Maxie, if you're going to get that far down the track, there's no point blocking.' Accordingly, once the ball was within range, I'd go for it. Following Dad's advice got me into enormous strife at times, but it was a lot of fun when I connected.

My last shot in first-class cricket was one of those, an attempted sixer off Bobby Holland at the Sydney Cricket Ground. It started in promising fashion but suddenly lost momentum and fell 20 paces the wrong side of the fence — straight down Johnny Dyson's throat at long on. I'd hit a few fours the same way in the first innings and was hoping for a farewell 50 but unfortunately it was not to be. The wily leggie had bought himself another victim.

Magic moments

1. Fastest Test hundreds

I WAS on the receiving end when diminutive West Indian Roy Fredericks blazed a century off just 71 balls at Perth in 1975. Roy started with a six off the second ball and never stopped throwing the bat. It was the fastest Test century ever recorded in Australia and remains the third fastest of all time.

The fastest and most recent 'miracle 100' was made by another West Indian, Viv Richards, who raced to 100 off just 56 balls against David Gower's England XI at Antigua in 1986. Viv lifted six sixes and thumped seven fours. Four of his sixes came from John Emburey's bowling. One was hit with just one hand. He made 110 not out before declaring. England lost the game and the series 5-0.

Between-the-wars all-rounder Jack Gregory holds the Australian record for the fastest Test century. He took just 67 balls against the South Africans in 1921-22.

Ian Botham has been the hardest hitting player of the modern era. He hit a record six sixes when he scored 118 at Manchester against Kim Hughes's 1981 Australians. I've only ever seen one comparable innings at international level, by New Zealander Lance Cairns who hit six sixes in a World Series Cup innings of 52 in front of 70,000 fans at the MCG in 1982-83. Four of the sixes were off the bowling of Hogg and Lillee. The faster they bowled, the harder big Lance hit!

West Indian opener Roy Fredericks blazed a century from just 71 balls at Perth in 1975. He was dynamic, threw the bat at everything and for hours had the Windies' run-rate kicking along merrily at nine and 10 an over. I remember it all too well — I was one of the bowlers on the receiving end.

How John Spooner of the Melbourne Age *heralded Viv Richards's super century.*

India's Sandeep Patil struck big, bad Bobby Willis for six fours in one over.

Ian Botham made his bats look like toothpicks. His hitting against the Australians on the '81 tour was remarkable.

FASTEST TEST HUNDREDS

	Balls faced	Opponent	Where	Year
Viv Richards (WI)	56	England	Antigua	1985-86
Jack Gregory (A)	67	S. Africa	Johannesburg	1921-22
Roy Fredericks (WI)	71	Australia	Perth	1975-76
Majid Khan (P)	74	New Zealand	Karachi	1976-77
Gilbert Jessop (E)	75	Australia	The Oval, London	1902
Bruce Taylor (NZ)	83	W. Indies	Auckland	1968-69
Ian Botham (E)	87	Australia	Leeds	1981
Ian Botham (E)	86	Australia	Manchester	1981

As a spectator, I've learnt to become enthralled when a batsman really goes for the bowling. I wasn't too pleased when batsmen like Clive Lloyd used to go after me, but I reckon you haven't earned your bowling spurs until you get a real hiding.

My contemporary, former England captain Bobby Willis, once had 24 hit off his bowling by Indian 'Sandy' Patil — and it was in a Test. One delivery was a no-ball, but it was still terrific batting.

2. Most runs off an over in Test cricket

HERE IS a list of the most number of runs off one Test over:

(a) Six-ball overs:
24 (4 6 2 6 6 leg bye) Andy Roberts, West Indies v England, Port-of-Spain, 1980-81 (off Ian Botham).
24 (4 4 4 [off a no-ball] 0 4 4 4) Sandeep Patil, India v England, Manchester, 1982 (Bob Willis).
24 (4 6 4 6 0 4) Ian Botham, England v NZ, The Oval, 1986 (Derek Stirling).
22 (1 1 6 6 2 6) Maurice Tate and Bill Voce, England v South Africa, Johannesburg, 1931-32 (Alfred Hall).
22 (0 6 4 0 6 6) Dick Motz, NZ v England, Dunedin, 1965-66 (David Allen).
22 (6 6 4 4 2 0) Dick Motz, NZ v India, Dunedin, 1967-68 (Erapalli Prasanna).
22 (6 6 6 0 2 2) Sylvester Clarke, WI v Pak, Faisalabad, 1980-81 (Nazir jnr).
22 (2 2 6 4 4 4) Ian Botham, Eng. v Australia, 'Gabba, 1986-87 (Merv Hughes).

(b) Eight-ball overs:
25 (6 6 0 6 1 6 0 0) Bert Sutcliffe and Bob Blair, New Zealand v South Africa, Johannesburg, 1953-54 (Hugh Tayfield).

THE MOST runs off an over in an Australian first-class match is 32 and the most from one over at Sheffield Shield level is 29 runs.

Former Australian captain Ian Craig, then 19, and Keith Carmody were responsible for the first feat while playing in Lindsay Hassett's testimonial match in Melbourne in January 1954. Craig (3 - - 6 6 0 6 6) and Carmody (- 4 1 - - - - -) hit Ian Johnson for 32 from an eight-ball over, representing Arthur Morris's XI versus Hassett's XI. They added 50 in eight minutes, Craig making 106 and Carmody 66. There was a happy ending to it all for 'Johnno' — he dismissed both men and finished with 4 for 182 from 18 overs.

Twenty-one-year-old David Hookes, on his way to his first Shield century, hit Victorian leg spinner Colin Thwaites for 29 in an eight-ball over at Adelaide in February 1977. He struck four sixes, a four and a single (6 0 6 6 0 6 4 1) and finished with 163 out of a team score of just 290.

Memories of my first Test innings

IT WAS 1972-73 and opening bat Keith Stackpole was out injured. The Australians were playing Pakistan in Melbourne and I was 'in', perhaps to save an airfare for anyone coming from interstate.

I had my baggy green cap and blazer fitted. It was magical stuff; it made the hair on the back of my neck stand up.

My Dad and I went through the side and agreed I was capable of replacing Stacky at the head of the list, but unfortunately nobody else did — Chappelli putting me in at nine.

We declared six down for about 500 odd and I didn't get a hit, but I did get to display my wares in the second dig. Three times I whacked Masood down the ground. I thought they were incredible shots — he was pretty quick, you know — and the cigar smokers in the Members seemed to be appreciative, too.

In came Thommo and he tried to emulate yours truly, but his cover drive only found square leg. I was halfway down the wicket trying to give him his first run in Test cricket but he bellowed 'No!' at the top of his voice. I'd never turned on a sixpence in my life. In fact, me changing direction mid-course is like seeing the Queen Mary berthing. I was stranded and by the time I had completed an 180-degree turn, the ball had been whipped back to the 'keeper and the umpire had a half-smile on his face. He knew I couldn't get back either!

Thommo just shrugged his shoulders, 'Sorry pal'. I was just 89 runs short of a 100, too!

My most embarrassing moment

IT WAS the second year of World Series Cricket and it was the closing stages of the fourth limited-over final, a day-nighter at VFL Park. The Windies already led the International Cup 2-1 but Australia had a great chance of levelling and forcing a fifth play-off game after scoring 240 and seeing the West Indians lose their first eight wickets for about 170.

Twenty-one-year-old David Hookes really went for our leggie, Col Thwaites, taking 29 off one of his overs at Adelaide in 1977.

Big-hitting West Indian Clive Lloyd showed me no mercy whatsoever— he took 20 runs from four balls before the lights went out...

David Hookes and I were to bowl out the last four overs with the West Indies needing 14 an over to win. We were pretty confident, even when golden-boy Hookes went for 22 off the fourth last one, cutting down the equation to two a ball.

Clive Lloyd was on strike to me for the start of the third last over. I steeled myself to concentrate on 'dot' balls and see if I could bowl a maiden over to the great man. From the first ball I bowled, Lloyd elegantly put his front foot down the track and went bang, straight over the sight screen for six!

I tried to pass it off as just one of those shots. What would a thinking bowler do? Okay, I'll go around the wicket and change the angle. That'll cramp him for room. I made sure it was short of a length and at the stumps. Once more that foot went down, the bat flashed across like a rapier and the ball went hurtling, first bounce, into the fence at mid-wicket.

There was a good crowd present and I could feel every eye on me. I changed back over the wicket, went out wider on the crease and again tried to cramp him. This time, he swivelled and hit me through mid-wicket for six. Sixteen off three balls! The Australians were looking stony-faced. I was wishing I could jump into a hole somewhere and hide!

I went back around the wicket and thought 'I'll bowl wide outside the off stump'. 'Supercat' Lloyd went down on one knee and clouted me through cover point, all the way along the ground for four. It was a marvellous, majestic shot. I had conceded 20 runs off four balls and from being likely to win, we were now in deep trouble.

Suddenly, however, all the lights went out. It was a 10.30 p.m. cut off, by demand of the local residents. Our match had gone overtime.

I don't know how many Lloydy would have taken off my last two deliveries. We all marched off — as best as we could, as it was pitch black — to learn that the West Indies had won on a superior run rate.

At some stage of his career, a bowler will have a nightmarish over he'll remember for the rest of his days. That was mine and I didn't even get to bowl the over out!

Nice guys do win

MANY CRICKETERS confuse gamesmanship with 'sledging'. Good bowlers are forever trying to create some seeds of doubt in the minds of the batsmen. It's what cricket is all about.

Shifting silly mid-off a step too close, an exaggerated appeal or a glare down the wicket when the guy has played and missed are just part of every good bowler's arsenal. It's part of the mental edge of the game.

Using four-letter words and saying derogatory things about a player's upbringing isn't the way to go. Some may claim it's a big boy's sport and anything goes, but the game's ethics, spirit and traditions are at stake.

There's another saying that nice guys don't win at sport or business. But there are enough examples around to disprove this theory.

The famous Dennis Lillee glare. Knowing Greigy, he wasn't too worried. 'Is that as fast as you can bowl FOT?' he was probably asking.

Nicknames and why they call me 'Tangles'

CRICKETERS ARE happiest when they are in groups, relaxing and chattering away after a game. Nicknames abound in these conversations.

I've been called 'Tangles' for so long that now I respond quicker to that name than I do to any of my given names, Maxwell, Henry or Norman!

I'd just turned 20 and had been picked for my first Victorian match when the Melbourne *Sun* printed the following caption under my photo: 'Melbourne's tangle-footed fast bowler Max Walker about to play his first Shield game.' The photo was from the thighs down and showed my legs crossed in classic pose. There was a little inset picture of my head in the top right-hand corner.

Suddenly my mates called me 'Tanglefoot'. This was shortened to 'Tangles' and now, if you're really good looking, some can get away with calling me 'Tang'.

There's been some rippers — Ian Chappell was 'Bertie', Brian Taber 'Herbie', Rick McCosker 'Bish', Jeff Thomson 'Two-up', Dougie Walters 'Bikki', Tony Greig 'Wash-peg', Chris Old 'Chilly', Geoff Arnold 'Horse' (his initials are G.G.).

Here's a selection of current nicknames:

Terry Alderman — 'Clem'.
David Boon — 'Daniel'.
Allan Border — 'A.B.'
Peter Faulkner — 'Flossy'.
Trevor Hohns — 'Cracka'.
Kim Hughes — 'Claggie'.
Merv Hughes — 'Hilly'.
Dean Jones — 'Ledge'.
Robbie Kerr — 'Guvna'.
Geoff Lawson — 'Henry'.
Ken Macleay — 'Slasher'.
John Maguire — 'Moose'.
Geoff Marsh — 'Swampy'.
Craig McDermott — 'Billy'.
Wayne Phillips — 'Flip' or 'Spaceman'.
Carl Rackemann — 'Mocca'.
Paul Reiffel — 'Pistol' or 'Chopper'.
Greg Ritchie — 'Fat Cat'.
Jamie Siddons — 'Sidchrome'.
Peter Sleep — 'Sounda'.
Steve Smith — 'Rags'.
Michael Taylor — 'Squizzy'.
Steve Waugh — 'Drobe'.
Dav Whatmore — 'Dave' or 'Gunga'.
Graeme Wood — 'Bazz'.

No one wanted to bat

MY INTRODUCTION to coaching youngsters came with Kerry Packer's involvement in World Series Cricket. The assembled kids, all 12- and 13-year-olds, were given brand new two-piece balls and I asked them how they went about trying to bowl an in-swinger and an out-swinger.

Most had an opinion. 'For the out-swinger, you tilt the ball towards first slip and run in close to the stumps,' said one. Others believed they should hold the ball across the seam and for the in-swinger, bowl wide of the popping crease.

From the mouths of ones so young, they were well-considered and logical arguments. But when it came to actually swinging the ball, only one or two could do it. At the all-important point of delivery, the kids simply were not in the correct position.

'It doesn't matter what it's like at the start of your run-up,' I told them. 'You must be comfortable when you let the ball go. You must be side on and be moving at pretty close to maximum speed.

'Seam up boys — and watch it swing.'

'You must also always bowl with the seam up. Your fingers must come right through, the wrist working just as hard as other parts of the body.'

I told them they had to unleash their momentum, from the energy conducted from the backs of their legs and calves and catapulted through their hips and ultimately, their shoulders.

I continued: 'Transmit all of that energy into the ball at the last point of contact when you deliver. Then, you've got a chance of swinging the ball.' The kids listened hard and quickly took up their positions in twos, about eight or nine metres away.

'Use the same grip for both the in-dipper and the away-swinger,' I told them. 'But whatever you do, remember one thing. Imagine there's a pin joint in your wrist. For the out-swinger, cock your wrist in towards your ear. Close your foot parallel to the crease. Drag down past the left leg, making sure that when you let go of the ball the seam is still vertical.

'By dragging down and following through as fully as possible, the ball will curve through the air.' The boys immediately started to bowl prodigious out-swingers.

'Now,' I said, quite pleased with the result, 'for the in-swinger, imagine that same pin joint, but this time cock it in the opposite direction, away from your ear. As you let the ball go, drag down vertically, without your arm flowing across your body as in the outie.'

With the seam vertical and following the pin-joint theory, the boys started to swing the ball 'in' — again in marked fashion. They were rapt. They didn't want to have a hit. They were now swinging the ball like the Test stars. Suddenly they were also closer to fulfilling their dreams.

OPQRSTUVWXYZ

Oops! I fail to recognise 'The Don'

JUST SOMETIMES in life, you wish you could become The Invisible Man and disappear without trace, especially if you happen to have dropped a catch in front of your Dad or done something equally embarrassing.

I found myself at a dinner at the Wentworth Hotel in Sydney to farewell the 1973 Australians to the Caribbean.

Talk about a 'who's who' of stars; they formed a reception line for us and I made a mental note to remember all their names. I knew Neil Harvey and there was Sammy Loxton, but who was this little bloke with the brushed-down Brylcreem hair? I thought he might have been a sponsor and asked him again for his surname. It was Sir Donald Bradman. No wonder he didn't talk to me much during my career!

But how was I to know? He didn't look anything like the oil painting hanging in the TCA room in Hobart!

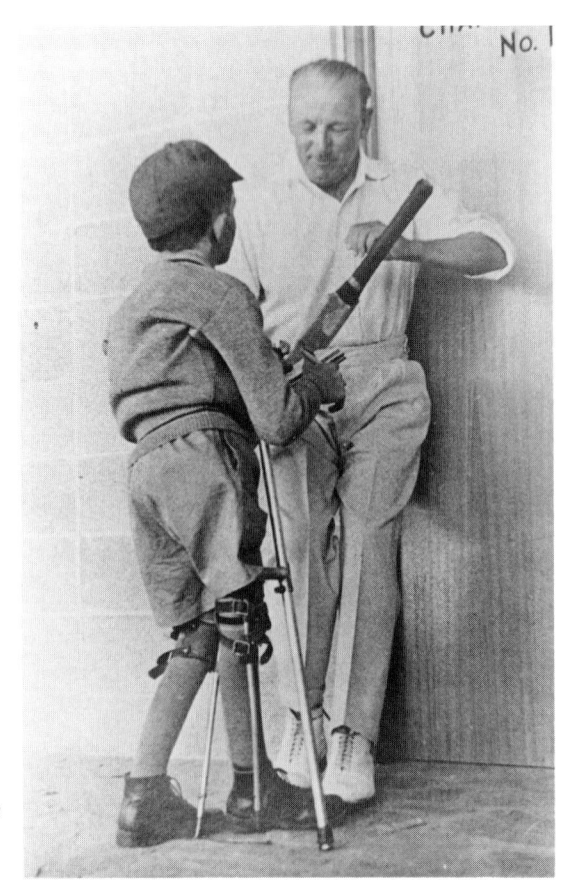

Sir Donald Bradman has probably signed more autographs than anyone alive. He's pictured delighting a young fan during his last match, the Prime Minister's XI v the MCC in 1962-63, at Manuka Oval. He made just four runs.

PQRSTUVWXYZ

Pranks from Dougie and other cricketers of my time

DOUGIE WALTERS was an incredible tourist. I'd room with him and he never cared much about sleep. About 4 o'clock most mornings you'd hear the sound of a can being opened and then a little red glow would appear, followed by a cough and a splutter.

There he was, sitting up in bed with his tinny and smoke, perfectly happy with his lot in life. 'You awake Tang?' he'd ask, knowing full well that you were, not that you'd let on. Boy, could he yak!

Dougie also happened to be the team's practical joker. Whichever town he was in, he'd hunt out the trick shops, looking for favourite devices like the exploding cigarette — for Ashley Mallett, who never bought his own — or a coin on a string which he loved to leave lying around dressing rooms, just waiting for a poor, unsuspecting soul to see. 'Rowdy' Mallett was a favourite target and Dougie got to know all his likes and dislikes, including his absolute aversion to spiders.

In the sixth Test at Melbourne in 1974-75, Mallett was called up for a long bowl, a rarity, as Thommo and Dennis Lillee had cleaned up most of the England batsmen in the early Tests. Walters managed to work himself around to mid-off, where he'd have last touch of the ball before throwing it back to Mallett.

Dougie Walters and Ross Edwards (left) hop into a few coldies after Doug had hit a century in a session versus the Poms in 1974. The 'Dungog Dasher' had a good season with both the bat and his practical jokery.

Surreptitiously removing an imitation plastic tarantula from his hip pocket and attaching chewing gum to the ball, Dougie casually threw the ball to Mallett, who grabbed for it, only to see the black beast. He screamed and, in front of a huge crowd, drop-kicked the ball well past the half-forward line!

During an England tour and within seconds of each other, he 'got' Mallett and Rod Marsh with exploding cigarettes. Dougie was rapt. 'This is what Test cricket is all about!' he'd laugh.

His *pièce de résistance* was his pound note fixed to the end of a nylon fishing line. He had a little coil spring in the palm of his hand and he'd throw the line out, press the gadget and the pound note would jump back into his hand! He had a ball with it, especially in the Poms' dressing room.

Dougie would casually sit back, clutching a beer, making sure he was in a position to keep an eye on the note. Derek Underwood once sighted it and had his hand about a foot away when Dougie went for the recoil button and back it flashed! Derek spluttered something about how he was just picking it up for Dougie but the room erupted.

Doug 'got' autograph hunters and all sorts of people in hotel foyers and in trains, but one day he met his match. We were having a drink in a little bar at the back of Lord's and nothing much was happening. As usual, Dougie had his little line out, just waiting for fresh prey. A paperboy came into the bar hollering the headlines in the *Evening News*. He saw the pound note as quick as a flash and Dougie's eyes lit up. You could see him 'willing' the boy into his trap.

The kid was smart: he walked straight over to it and put his foot down hard. Panicking, Dougie went for the button, the line snapped, the kid bent over, picked up the note, stuck it in his pocket and walked out whistling!

Dougie loved cards and often preferred to remain inside when the others went out for a short practice. Before the Guyana Test in the West Indies, Ian Chappell told Dougie that he might do a bit of bowling in recognition of his 4 for 9 against the Youth XI in Barbados. There's nothing that makes a batsman happier than hearing from his skipper that he's going to get a bowl the next day, so Dougie worked out harder than any of us in the nets. Next day he discovered he was pretty sore in the shoulders from all this unaccustomed exercise.

On the morning of the match, we went out to the nets for a half-hour session while Doug, as usual, remained behind in the dressing room, with his pack of cards. When we came back, sweating profusely, Chappelli went up to Doug and enquired if he, too, should loosen up. 'After all, we might be bowling first,' said Ian.

Doug pondered for a few seconds and then conceded that it might be a good idea if he worked some of the stiffness out. With this as his objective, he walked to the dart board, extracted half a dozen darts, walked back, flexed his muscles, aimed and grouped the six darts around the bullseye. 'That's that,' said Doug. 'I'm loose. Now I suppose I'd better get some batting practice.' He proceeded to shuffle the cards and deal himself another hand of patience.

Perhaps it was an unorthodox approach, but we did bowl first, and Doug took 5 for 66, followed with a chanceless 81 and we won by 10 wickets to clinch the series!

Queen's Park and an unforgettable victory

CRICKET IS the best common denominator I know. It's a great leveller, enjoyed by people of all ages. Australia's Prime Minister, Bob Hawke, has a game, and while he doesn't hook as well as he ought these days, he's a great enthusiast and on his last appearance at the MCG in the annual Politicians—Crusaders game, scored 30-odd in good style before being caught by my co-author, cricket writer Ken Piesse.

'First time I've been caught out by a journalist in 25 years!' quipped Bob. Cricket's like that. It's humorous and players and teams build a terrific bond. As players get closer and closer, they become very hard to toss.

It's the same in football. The unity and camaraderie among the players has to be seen to be believed. 'Crackers' Keenan tells the story of Malcolm Blight, who played in North Melbourne's first two VFL premierships in 1975 and 1977. He was returning home to coach in South Australia and was flying out on Christmas Eve.

Unknown to him, all his old football mates — including the guys who had played in the premierships — went out to Tullamarine airport to give him a surprise farewell. They wanted to say goodbye to their mate, even if it was Christmas Eve. Malcolm couldn't handle it. He cried.

Australia's Prime Minister, Bob Hawke, didn't always hook as well as he should have.

The Australian cricket team of the early '70s was noted for its closeness. There were only two or three places up for grabs over a three- or four-year period and we developed a total team commitment. It was go for broke in every match. We never talked about losing; we expected to win and played like it.

The bond between players was our biggest single strength during the time we were the best cricket team in the world. Our spirit helped to create incredible wins from the darkest situations. The shining example came at Port-of-Spain, Trinidad, in the third Test of the 1972-73 tour. It was a game we had no right to win.

With the series nil-all after two draws, the Windies went to lunch on the final day secure in the knowledge that they needed just 66 runs to win. Lawrence Rowe had broken his ankle while fielding and couldn't bat, but there were still five other wickets in hand.

The West Indians were understandably confident. Steel bands were queued up in trucks outside the ground, just waiting for the end when they could come onto the ground to help share in the victory spoils. Things looked black for us — it was a great deck, Alvin Kallicharran was in top form and, with four hours to go, the target of 66 runs seemed a formality. They just had to win.

Ian Chappell had given us a bit of a 'gee-up' and out we went again, determined to give it our best shot and if we had to lose, we intended to go down fighting.

I don't know if little 'Kalli' got stuck into the curried goat, fried rice and the 25 varieties of blowflies at the break, but he was away with the fairies on resumption and to my very first ball — angled wide of his off stump — he dabbed at it, got a big edge and 'Bacchus' Marsh took the catch. Last man 91. Team score 5 for 268. Sixty-six runs still needed to win.

Suddenly we all stepped taller. The danger man was out. Perhaps we could get out of jail after all… The game's fortunes were to swing dramatically during that session. 'Skully' O'Keeffe got a couple of wickets, I bowled the local mystery spinner Inshan Ali and suddenly the West Indies were 'nine-for'.

Last man Lance Gibbs came out to bat and, on entering the Queen's Park oval, he slowly and very deliberately 'crossed' himself. About 100 fans hanging out of the barbed-wire freedom stand at the far end started chanting 'Arr-men, Arr-men, Arr-men'. The Windies still needed another 45 and O'Keeffe and Terry Jenner had been making the ball spin like a top.

I was bowling tightly in tandem with O'Keeffe and when the 'Arr-men' chant started, I even lost the skip in my run-up. I'm not saying it was anything like Michael Holding's run to the wicket but it was *almost* rhythmic. It was incredible out there.

Gibbs was at the non-striker's end when O'Keeffe hit the edge of Keith Boyce's bat. It flew to Ian Chappell at slip and Boyce was out. He couldn't believe it. He looked up in the air, shook his head, stared at the wicket, looked up in the air again and slowly trudged off. We'd come from nowhere. We'd won.

The injured Keith Stackpole came running out onto the ground. He'd been hit in the face by Kallicharran while fielding at short leg earlier in the game and had stitches on both the inside and outside of his jaw. He was a real mess, but there was no denying his or our joy after it dawned that we'd done the impossible and pinched a game that was never going to be ours.

Skully didn't know whether to laugh or cry. Billy Jacobs, our team manager,

'Boyce couldn't believe it. He looked up in the air, shook his head, stared at the wicket and trudged off. We'd come from nowhere. We'd won…' A 'V' for victory sign from Kerry O'Keeffe; 'Marshy' is already on 'Cloud Nine' over our unforgettable victory.

The touring team which stole the Trinidad Test: Back row, left to right: Johnny Watkins, 'T.J.' Jenner, 'Fergie' Massie, yours truly, Johnny Benaud, 'Skully' O'Keeffe, 'Bomber' Hammond and Rosco Edwards. Front row, left to right: Dougie Walters, 'Redders', 'Chappelli', Bill Jacobs (manager), 'Stacky', 'Bacchus' Marsh and Greg Chappell.

was also on the ground jigging up and down. None of us could believe it.

Our skipper, Chappelli, had a lot to do with that win. A few breaks hadn't gone our way earlier in the day and a few had become downcast. His lunchtime 'bake' snapped us all back to reality: 'We were a good team. Let's go and show it.'

The fielding in that mid-afternoon session was out of this world. Queen's Park had little grass on it and many of our fielders had bloodied elbows and knees from diving on balls which otherwise would have gone through to the fence. It remains a red-letter day in my life. Winning isn't everything, but it sure beats losing!

The mates you make in cricket are your mates for life: 10 of us walk down to congratulate Jeff Thomson (out of picture) on taking his first Test wicket of the 1975 series, at Edgbaston. From left: Rod Marsh (back to camera), Doug Walters, Ian Chappell, Ross Edwards, Alan Turner, Rick McCosker, Ashley Mallett, yours truly, Greg Chappell and Dennis Lillee.

RSTUVWXYZ

'Redders' and my favourite bat

TREASURE YOUR favourite bats, no matter how old or decrepit they may become. An old bat is like an old friend and it's a sad day when you have to withdraw one from active service. A good bat means so much. You tend to be more comfortable and 'in control' at the crease. With a less-familiar blade, it's usually harder to settle.

One day up in Queensland, I was presented with a bat made of red gum. It was a dead-set seven-pound job. It was huge; it had no springs or anything. They had nailed half a cricket ball to it. I would loved to have brought it home but it was just too heavy. I would have been up for excess baggage!

Times have changed and I'm sure today's bats don't last as long as they once did. Nowadays, youngsters like to sport the cherry-red marks of conquest on their bats; in our day we would rub off any marks with very light sandpaper and, with an oily rag, run over the blade once or twice — carefully steering clear of the splice.

My 'old faithful' was a Stuart Surridge laminated-edge job. It was a revolutionary bat for the time. It was willow like any other, but had hardwood edges. I picked one up brand spanking new and took it into a Test match at the Oval one day.

The first ball I faced, from Derek Underwood, went one bounce over the pickets at square leg. It fairly smoked away and without any effort. The second one went the same way. I looked lovingly at that bat and said: 'What a little beauty you are!'

Duncan Fearnley hand-crafting one of his bats at his English headquarters. I bet you the one he's working on doesn't weigh seven pounds like the Big Bertha I was presented with in Queensland!

It was just so good. All my life I'd been searching for the perfect stick and the ball just cannoned off this little baby. It went everywhere with me. I even found myself coming in at eight — and quite rightly, too, according to my Dad, Big Max — after my scintillating 32 batting at No. 9 for Victoria against Thommo and Co. in the opening Sheffield Shield game of the season!

We got to Adelaide, halfway through the Test series with the Windies, and someone went and knocked off Ian Redpath's Stuart Surridge bat. Redders was inconsolable. He'd made a century with it two Tests previously in Melbourne and as a long-standing 'SS man', wasn't going to use anything else.

It was the first morning of the fifth Test and we were batting. Redders looked wildly around the room, searching for a bat carrying the familiar SS stickers. I saw his plight, unzipped my bag and came across with mine and said: 'Mate, it's a long handle and pretty heavy, but you're welcome to it — for *this* match only.'

He'd never used a long handle before and eyed it pretty dubiously. But he picked it up and with a relieved expression said 'It's not that heavy Tang' and out he marched.

He had already borrowed my thigh-pad — he used it as a ribcage guard — and, with his elite Geelong schooling pedigree, I thought there would be no problem reclaiming my gear. It was a top bat, that Surridge. It picked up beautifully and with three or four grips on it, was ideal.

Redders was to make 103 and 65 in that game, actually hitting the only two sixes of his Test career (it had taken him 65 Tests!). He was as pleased as punch and begged me to extend my generosity. He was to use it for the rest of the series, finishing with another 'ton' in Melbourne, his third of the series.

He was under threat to return it, especially if he happened to still be 'in' when yours truly marched in. But of course he wouldn't. He started to bat with it for Vic-

Redders leans on my Stuart Surridge bat as he and 'Bish' McCosker share a joke in Sydney, 1975-76.

David Hookes and his 'old faithful' — it was dry, chips were lifting and cord was wrapped around it — but he wouldn't swap it, even for the historic Centenary Test of 1977.

toria, too. Once I joined him at the wicket, armed with a new Rapier — and some hankies in my pocket to protect my bare thigh — expecting Red to do the right thing and swap. As I neared the crease, I tried a little eyeball contact but nothing happened. He had his back to me and refused to look me in the eye!

I reckon he went to bed with that bat in the end, but if I'd made three 'tons' in a series, I would have too!

Legend has it that Redders still has my beloved weapon and gives it pride of place in his antique shop at Geelong...not that he'd tell me. Whenever he knows I'm coming, he hides it. He never told me, either, what happened to 'his' ribcage protector! Possession is nine-tenths of the law!

David Hookes is also a great one for hoarding — and restoring — his best bats. He hit five centuries in a row to make the 1977 Centenary Test side, using a battered, old thing which appeared to be held together only by some bruised pig skin around its middle. It was dry, chips were lifting and cord was wrapped around it. But as persuasive as the Gray-Nicolls bat people were, he wouldn't change it for the historic match and ended up making a memorable half-century which including five consecutive fours off the bowling of England captain Tony Greig.

The following season, after being dismissed cheaply a couple of times with a new blade, he went back to his 'Real McCoy', did an incredible rebind job on it and started using it successfully again.

Another South Australian, Peter Sleep, has a similar theory and aims to use his 'old faithful' until it splits. He made 90 with it in the 1987-88 Christmas Test versus

66 *Hooked on Cricket*

the Kiwis and has successfully thwarted all offers from Gray-Nicolls to update.

There have been some weird and wonderful bats on show during my career. Once in the Caribbean, I borrowed Rodney Marsh's 'Big Bertha' and, although I made only 20 and would have batted for less than half an hour, my wrists were sore for days afterwards. It weighed a ton (or tonne) — and surely approached the huge bats used by the acknowledged modern-day 'hurricane' hitters, England's Ian Botham and New Zealand's Lance Cairns.

Dennis Lillee tended to chop and change bat manufacturers a bit and for several much-publicised weeks — basically as a money-making exercise — he experimented with an aluminium bat. His revolutionary 'Combat' bat was basically a bit of cold water pipe, combined with a few welded supportive ribs which had been encased in aluminium.

The original version of his bat had an open toe and prankster Doug Walters would stand it upside down and use it as an ash tray, mostly when Dennis wasn't looking, but sometimes when he was!

A good marketing man at heart, Dennis felt its introduction should be made at Test level, and what better opportunity than the opening Australia—England Test of the 1979-80 summer…and in front of his home Perth crowd at that!

Dennis was not-out overnight (using a conventional bat) after Friday's opening day. In he went on Saturday morning, armed with his radical, aluminium bat, and played three balls from Ian Botham before he attempted a death-or-glory off-drive — and sent the ball skidding back past 'Both'.

'*A huge argument developed.*' Dennis Lillee and Mike Brearley had never exchanged Christmas cards and nothing changed after the aluminium bat incident, as this terrific Bill Mitchell cartoon shows.

With all the effort which had gone into it, it should have probably gone for a 'seven' but it just lobbed short of the long-off boundary and the batsmen ran three. There had been a very strange thud of bat connecting with ball and England captain Mike Brearley immediately complained, saying Dennis might ruin the ball with his bat and could he please exchange it for a more traditional blade?

I don't think Dennis and Mike had ever exchanged Christmas cards and a huge argument developed before the wild colonial boy stalked angrily towards the pavilion. Twelfth man Rodney Hogg jogged on with some more suitable wooden bats but Dennis didn't like any of them and marched off, still with his aluminium bat under his arm!

The crowd was in uproar and the players didn't know what to think. Skipper Greg Chappell gently explained it was probably best if he did change it, so Dennis started fossicking for his old favourite, of the more-acceptable willow variety!

But the 'fun' wasn't finished yet. Dennis's great buddy Rodney Marsh interrupted, asking Dennis if he was really going to let 'a bloody Pom and two umpires' ruin his bat-making career. 'Fancy that mate,' said Rod, with as straight a face as he could muster, 'you must be getting soft…I thought you told me there could be big bucks to be made with that bat!'

With skipper Chappell telling his 'keeper not to inflame the situation, or words to that effect, Lillee, still with smoke coming from his ears, said 'Yeah, you're right, Bacchus' and marched back on, still with his aluminium bat!

This time the dressing room broke up in fits of laughter. Lillee was arguing again out in the middle and this time Chappell came out with a bat and told Dennis that in his opinion the off-drive for three would have been worth four if it had been struck with a conventional blade. Dennis could see sense in that. Like all tail-enders, he's proud of his run-making ability. But as a last act, he threw the offending bat into the outfield before taking his place again at the crease. Play had been interrupted for 10 minutes — and all over a silly bit of cold water pipe!

The upshot was that cricket authorities implemented a new law which outlawed all bats other than those made of wood.

How Melbourne cartoonist George Haddon saw the aluminium bat incident.

S TUVWXYZ

Self-made champions

THIS MIGHT surprise you, but our greatest Test match bowler, Dennis Lillee, was as self-made a champion as there'll ever be. At the start of his career, he was skin and bones. He reminded me of one of those comic book 'weakies' who gets sand kicked in his face at the beach by an athletic, muscular guy who then walks away with the pretty girl.

Unlike his fast bowling partner, Jeff Thomson, who was a sporting 'natural', Dennis had to work at his game. Initially he could bowl fast but only for short periods. By building his body and stamina he became a true champion, the greatest fast bowler Australia has seen.

Lillee's fitness allowed him to fulfil a dream in 1988 and play English county cricket, continuing a comeback which had seen him play the last half of the 1987-88 season with Tasmania. He even took a wicket with his first comeback delivery, a *Boys' Own Annual* re-entry into major cricket; a performance we'd come to expect of a player of Dennis's stature.

In his first county game in England he took six wickets in an innings. Again the cricket world was hardly surprised. Such was the standard Dennis had set.

Another West Australian and former Australian cricketer, Ross Edwards, was

The batsman's view of another Lillee thunderbolt. He must be Australia's greatest fast bowler, a real self-made champion.

Would you kick sand in this young man's face? The teenage Lillee, all bone and sinew but little muscle, had a fierce determination to become the world's best — he succeeded.

No one worked harder at all aspects of his game than 'Sandgroper' Ross Edwards. He had a few weaknesses — off-spin bowling and port after dinner — but was a fabulous tourist.

also inspirational. Ross was a first-rate wicket-keeper but struggled for a regular State spot as first Gordon Becker and then Rod Marsh were picked ahead of him.

'Rosco's' answer was to turn himself into a cover fielder. He rigged up special netting in his backyard and for hours on end, most days of the week, would fire throws and returns at a single stump. He became one of the top-line cover fielders this country has seen. He was another who played well within his limitations. His only vices were port and pipe tobacco, and he enjoyed both in copious amounts.

Ross enjoyed being at the 'other' end in long partnerships. He'd love to scamper a single which would enable a Dougie Walters or one of the Chappells to get back on strike. He'd sit back and enjoy the spectacle, making sure he ran like the wind to avoid the run out. If he was in a 100-run partnership and had made 35 or 40, he'd done his bit and was happy.

Dennis Lillee and Ross Edwards were also sticklers for wearing the right gear and *looking* like cricketers. I can't emphasise this factor too much. Keep your gear neat and presentable, your equipment in good shape and you'll be better off.

Lazy cricketers are the ones who are forever borrowing gear, rarely have their boots whitened and don't quite look the part. It may be a small part of the game for some, but as the old saying goes — you can't be a cricketer if you don't look like a cricketer.

Schooldays

AS A graduate of Landsdowne Crescent State School in Hobart, I keenly remember our cricket matches, before school, at recess and again at lunchtime, each day, five days a week.

I don't remember too much else about the school or my scholastic record, but I remember the elation of being able to bat through a whole 'day's play'. It was no mean feat, remembering there'd be 40 to 50 fielders around you and four or five bowlers operating in tandem. Despite the keen opposition, I had my fair share of hits and developed into an all-rounder.

If I did get out quickly, I found I could usually get back in again by knocking over the old garbage bin we used as a wicket with a fast one aimed at the batsman's legs. The bin was invitingly wide. If a kid happened to miss the ball and wasn't bowled, my 'lbw' shout was usually upheld!

We used to play on a concrete wicket at a place called 'The Rec'. There were prickle bushes at one end and it was pretty rough. I made the school team in grade four and ended up being captain of footy and cricket in grade six. I was a big fish in a little pool. But suddenly there was a huge turnaround.

I found myself at The Friends' School, North Hobart, a good co-educational school — not that I cared; my priorities were with cricket, not girls!

On my first day at school I discovered that I should have been wearing short socks and trousers and an open-necked shirt. Typical me, I wore long socks with the short pants, complete with shirt and tie. I was a laughing stock.

I counted off the minutes before recess, hoping there'd be a game of cricket going to take my mind off my first-day blues. There was and, despite all the ribbing which was continuing, I grabbed a ball, paced out my longest run and sprinting in, bowled the first like the wind.

Dean Jones: 'Sometimes I didn't have enough respect for the bowler…'

With my second ball, I hit the old rubbish bin which acted as our stumps. The batsman was out bowled and I was in!

I remember holding that old bat tightly, telling myself not to get out. It was a terrible old bat, cracked and with some wood missing in the middle. But it had a good pick-up and I stayed in all recess and lunch time. None of the boys could get me out. As the bell rang, a big bloke came over to me with some mates. His name was John Neilson and he was captain of the under-13 cricket team.

'Would you like to play in our side?' said Johnny.

'Sure,' I said, thrilled to be asked. No one mentioned my long socks and I'd discarded the tie long before so it wouldn't get in my eye while batting. 'Sure,' I said to Johnny again. 'Sure, I'll play.'

We became bosom buddies. He was best man at my wedding and I was best man at his. Not only is cricket a great leveller, it leads to life-long friendships.

Shorten the pitch!

LADS SHOULD be able to use a smaller cricket ball, weighing less than normal, and have the opportunity of bowling on a 15- or 18-yard pitch. They shouldn't have to bowl all 22 yards — or with a full-size ball — until they reach their teens.

Stars-talk

ONE OF my recommendations for young cricketers is to read as widely as possible, keep a scrapbook and cut out interesting stories, particularly those where cricketers talk about technique and theory. I'm forever collecting newspaper clippings, much to the dismay of the kids, especially if their favourite comic strip happens to be on the back!

I present a few of them, gleaned from present-day players:
- Australian Test batsman **Dean Jones**, on playing a 'percentage' game and

respecting a bowler: 'I really try to make the most of it when I get a start now,' he says. 'I'm also starting now to play more of a percentage game, revolving around my own team's needs rather than playing my own sort of game.

'The main thing I've realised is that guys can bowl a good ball. Sometimes I didn't have enough respect for the bowler but I now know that he's capable of bowling a good ball to you when you're nine, 99 or 159. You have to be wary and on guard.

'Guys tend to think once they get to 30 they should start playing shots. But it's the time when you've really got to work harder. When I was in England for the Rest of the World match, I was chatting with Sunny Gavaskar, the great Indian, and he said to me: "A lot of guys like hitting the ball and hitting fours but I just enjoy batting and all its facets."

'That's what I've had to realise...I get a lot of pleasure in hitting fours and sixes and big shots but I also enjoy keeping out a good bowler and making that bowler bowl well at me.'

• Australian Under-25 wicket-keeper, Victorian **Michael Dimmatina**: 'You can learn a lot from what the successful people say and think. They can be from any walk of life, not just cricketers. David Boon was struggling last season (1986-87) but refused to worry too much. He said the runs would come, and they did. He had the belief in his own ability.'

• Australian left-arm opening bowler **Bruce Reid**: 'Each day I write down how I feel and what I'm thinking before and after a performance. Now, on the eve of a match, I go back through the data and look for a good performance. I then try and adopt the same frame of mind and procedures for the next day.

'It has worked very well so far, especially with my concentration. I find I'm able to keep my mind on the job for much longer periods. Now I keep my front arm up

Bruce Reid: 'I try to be positive and continually remind myself I'm playing for my country.' (England's Allan Lamb is caught behind off Reid, Christmas Test at the MCG, 1986; Botham is the non-striker.)

in its proper place before delivery and I'm following through as I should do on every ball.

'Also, instead of saying to myself: "Gee I want to go home" when I am really flat, I try to be positive and continually remind myself I'm playing for my country. Best of all, I'm learning to enjoy myself more.'

• **Dean Jones**, again: 'I've been working on a couple of changes in the nets. I'm trying to play the ball a little later and to stop moving around before the bowler lets the ball go. I now stand very still.'

• Australian leg spinner **Peter Sleep**, on bowling with his eyes closed: 'Before a Test in Adelaide, Richie Benaud offered some advice to Greg Matthews and myself, on how a bowler can make sure he is bowling rhythmically. He got us to bowl, the whole run-up, everything, with our eyes closed. It was great. I discovered that if I concentrated hard enough, I could bowl the right line and length even with my eyes closed.'

• **David Boon**, after making 103 against England at Adelaide in 1986-87, after a bad run of 'outs': 'It was worrying, even depressing but if I was going to recover I had to be confident when I went out [to bat]. My teammates helped me so much in this area. For example 'Mo' [Greg Matthews] kept telling me before the game that Adelaide was my turf. Mentally I was different today. Last night I went through in my mind all the good knocks I've had in my career. I did the same over breakfast.'

• Australian batsman **Mike Veletta** on some pre-innings psychology: 'On the advice of a Western Australian sports psychologist, I now concentrate on a set routine in preparation for each innings. I make sure I relax as much as possible. You have just got to bring yourself down that cog or two, so you can perform at your best.'

Peter Sleep: 'I discovered that if I concentrated hard enough, I could bowl the right line and length even with my eyes closed.'

Sons of famous players Rod Marsh and Kim Hughes get in some practice at the WACA. Will they be our Test openers for the summer season of 2008/9?

Start 'em young

I'VE ALWAYS been a great believer in starting 'em young and how about the enthusiasm of these two young men — one aged six, the other five and half. I came across their photo on the front page of the *West Australian* newspaper of 19 March 1988, and immediately thought I'd seen them both before…

I was right — the dark-haired lad is Geoff Marsh's son, Sean, while the blondie is Kim Hughes's boy, Bradley. Photographer Barry Baker sighted them playing their version of a Test match during the 1987-88 Sheffield Shield final. I'm not sure who won but it looks like they had a lot of fun doing it. Great stuff!

Superstitions

TODAY'S TEST cricketers are just as superstitious as we ever were. Current Test captain Allan Border doesn't shave immediately before or during a game. Fast bowler Michael Whitney gives the ball a kiss before he bowls his first delivery of a game.

South Australian Michael Haysman, who had such a brilliant tour of South Africa with the Australian rebel team in 1986-87, likes listening to the music of Grace Jones before he bats. If he makes a big score, he won't wash his cricket clothes between innings. He'd be in trouble if his name was Bradman!

Like Border, I never shaved before a game, but neither did Dennis Lillee or 'Two-up' Thomson. It wasn't superstition as much as commonsense — you needed the extra protection being out under that hot summer sun for long periods.

When padding up, I always put my left pad on first and would feel strange if I did anything else. I had a reddish, paisley, short-sleeved shirt which used to go well with denim, flared jeans and I'd wear this favourite shirt until it could virtually walk to the cleaners by itself!

These were the days when we were dubbed 'the ugly Australians' and tracksuits and runners were part of our touring wardrobe instead of blazers and grey trousers. We would religiously use the same cricket clothing with which we'd been successful until the gear literally came apart at the seams. The shirts we had on when we'd taken a few wickets or made a few runs would be hung up at the end of a day and put back on again the next morning! Anything to keep the luck going…

Michael Whitney, pictured in his first Test series with Dennis Lillee (versus England in 1981), has become renowned for his habit of kissing the ball before his first delivery of a game.

I'd stick with the same pair of boots until I got 'none-for'. Only then would I attempt to start breaking in some new ones. While the wickets were coming, I'd just tape up the old ones and keep going.

Victorian and Australian teammate Richie Robinson had this antique pair of wicket-keeping inners and, despite their shocking state, he refused to give them up. One day on the World Series Cricket Cavaliers tour, someone knocked them off and burnt them in a Vegemite jar. Richie was very upset; there was no way he felt as confident without them.

Some 'Shark'-like theory

TOP AUSTRALIAN golfer Greg 'Shark' Norman says sport is like a pendulum — your fortunes swing one way and then the other.

My theory has always been that if you bowl straight enough, well enough for long enough, you'll get wickets. Don't get preoccupied by people saying you're doing 'this, this and that' wrong. Dissect the advice carefully, keeping what you feel is suitable to your game and ignore the rest.

In a Test match you have to be able to stand up longer than the bloke at the other end. Have a plan and try to force the batsman into making an error or a false shot he would not normally contemplate. It may take you three, or even six maiden overs, with your opponent all the time champing at the bit to play a drive through the invitingly-wide gap at cover.

Stick to your plan, bottle him up and and refuse to give him even a sniff of a half-volley, suitable for his pet shot. Sooner or later, he's going to try and break the shackles. Perhaps his shot will be out of character and he'll make a mistake. If you bowl to a plan, you have a chance.

Maintain your two slips and two gullies and have a shortish cover for the 'spooned' drive. The trap is set. The batsman knows it. So do you. You must have the control and the aggression. It's either him or you. You know if you bowl poorly for three or four overs, you're not in the hunt. But if you bowl well, as good a batsman as he may be, you're a big chance to force him into an error.

He might go for a slower ball, wide of the off stump and hit it straight down short cover's throat. If he does, you know you're on, at least for one more over!

Greg Norman: 'Sport is like a pendulum — your fortunes swing one way and then the other.'

Tales of 'Tiny', Big Wes and 'Fiery' Boycott

I WAS among a huge group of kids watching every move the 1960-61 West Indian cricketers made at practice at the TCA. We'd imitate their walk, their actions, everything.

Every now and again, a ball would fly over the fence and we'd rush to retrieve it, grateful for the opportunity. When the match started, a lot of us would congregate at fine leg, autograph books at the ready, hoping the resting fast bowlers would stop and have a chat between deliveries.

When big Wes Hall smiled at us, we thought it was Christmas. I thought he must have been at least seven feet tall. Wes asked us how we were going and later I was to get his autograph after sneaking in the lavatory window of the old pavilion.

Wes was terrific with the kids and ever since then, I've always felt it's important for players to communicate across the fence and become involved with the crowd. It doesn't break your concentration but it does make a memorable day for the fans.

It took the dour Yorkshireman Geoff Boycott until his last tour of Australia to realise there was a lot of fun to be had down at third man. He had a 'bad guy' reputation and knew it, but suddenly he relaxed, held conversations with the boys in Bay 13, smiled at junior, signed an autograph or two, had a sip of a drink and enjoyed the company. When he got a good throw back, the crowd would roar their appreciation, and 'Fiery' would turn around and acknowledge with a bow. The people loved it. 'He's unreal that Boycott,' they'd say, 'he said this and that. I offered him a drink and he signed my autograph book.'

They'd go along the next time, hoping Boycott would again be fielding in front of them. His positive reaction to the crowd support actually bought more people in — and that's the way it should be all the time. Crowds should be catered for.

'He's unreal that Boycott...I offered him a drink and he signed my autograph book.'

lost its shine, but also had bits of leather hanging off it. I was bowling into the wind and the second new ball was still a long way off.

The sensational West Indian run-rate had rarely been seen at this level of cricket — and there I was, with what was left of the cherry, hoping for a miracle. What you have to say to yourself in these situations is:

- Don't look at the scoreboard. It's irrelevant. If you have the ball in your hand, you are just one ball away from taking a wicket. (However, sometimes it takes a long time for that wicket-taking ball to occur!)
- You also have to say to yourself that you are better equipped than the batsman down the other end. Never think: 'Gee, it'd be nice *if* I could take a wicket.' You say: 'Yes, I *can* take a wicket.'
- Close your eyes and imagine getting the bloke down the other end out. Mentally rehearsing your next action has been used successfully in all sorts of sports, such as by leading golfers. Before they make a crucial putt, they go through the steps required and actually imagine themselves making that putt.

It's like having to bowl to Viv Richards in top form. It's not a matter of marking out your run-up and then asking yourself what you are going to do. You should have bowled to Viv over-after-over in your sleep the night before, working out your match strategies and contingency plans. Similarly, you should 'bowl' to everyone in the opposition side before it actually happens.

- Ensure that your field is carefully placed. See where the 'enemy' is scoring freely and block off those avenues.

In that Perth Test, it was no use me bowling with four slips and a gully as no one had been able to move the ball previously and within a few deliveries I knew I couldn't either. I may have been bowling dead straight but at least I could implement all my much-practised variations.

I was getting no assistance in the air or off the pitch, so I tried doing a few other things. I bowled one wide, another from 23 yards, one closer to the stumps, one

No wonder I'm smiling, with two super-quicks on either side of me. FOT, yours truly and Thommo — a good Australian threesome if I may say so myself!

fuller and one quicker. All the time I worked at changing my grip, picking at the seam, anything to cause the ball to do something different so the batsman would have to think a bit.

Perhaps he could even be enticed into mishitting the ball and be caught. That was my plan and that's the way I tried to bowl.

I didn't have the natural pace or brute strength of a Thommo or a Lillee. I couldn't intimidate anyone with a bouncer — even my sister used to hook me for sixes in the backyard at Mum's! But a lot of sweat and brainpower later, I'd finished with 2 for 99 from my 17 overs which, while hardly flattering, wasn't too bad considering the scoreline of 585.

Postscript: We all took heaps of stick that memorable mid-December day. Dennis Lillee went for six an over, Thommo seven, 'Gus' Gilmour eight and me five. 'Rowdy' Mallett was the most economical, conceding less than four an over, but it was little consolation — he didn't get a wicket, his 26 overs costing 103 runs!

Ten tall tales but true

1. I NEVER scored a century in first-class cricket. My best was 78 not out in my very last Test match against England at the Oval in 1977. Thommo and I added 30-odd for the last wicket.

Wisden Cricketers' Almanack reported: 'Walker, badly missed by Brearley at 19, put on exactly 100 (with Malone) mainly by reputable strokemaking… Walker finished unbeaten with his highest score, 78 (10 fours) made in two hours, 20 minutes.' I thought Mr Wisden was being a bit hard on old Mike. I'd given it a bit of a thumping and even Superman would have struggled to catch it!

But I'm dirty on Thommo — he went out on me and I was denied the century I so richly deserved!

2. OLD-TIME Victorian spinner 'Chuck' Fleetwood-Smith said he wished he'd been hit for another four during that incredible Test at the Oval in 1938 when England scored a massive 7 for 903 declared.

'Chuck' Fleetwood-Smith started as a right-arm fast bowler at school, but after breaking his arm, experimented with left-arm wrist spinners and was so successful that he played for Australia in the 1930s ahead of legendary Clarrie Grimmett.

'My figures were 1 for 298,' Fleetwood-Smith told friends. 'If there'd been one more fourer, I would have become the only man ever to concede 300 runs in a Test innings!'

According to my dusty, old 1939 *Wisden*, Len Hutton scored his famous 364, breaking Bradman's record of 334. When chirpy wicket-keeper Arthur Wood was out for 53, with the score at 7 for 876, he muttered: 'Trust me to get out in a crisis.'

Fleetwood-Smith wasn't the only expensive bowler in that mammoth innings — Bill 'Tiger' O'Reilly returned 3 for 178 and Mervyn Waite 1 for 150. They bowled almost 250 overs between them.

I feel tired just looking at that amazing scoresheet!

3. FLEETWOOD-SMITH bowled an incredible 87 (six-ball) overs in that huge England innings, but it's not the record. The most overs sent down by an Australian occurred at Old Trafford in 1964 when Queensland finger spinner Tom Vievers bowled 95.1 overs (returning 3 for 155) against the Poms. 'Chuck' bowled left-arm wrist spinners, a rarity today.

4. AT VICTORIA'S historic gold-mining town of Bendigo in 1985, Wedderburn's 'Big Jim' Steel hit eight consecutive sixes on his way to 82 from 23 balls against Gisborne. The next batsman in, Mick Steel, Jim's cousin, scored 52 including five sixes. The unlucky bowler to feel the force of Jim's assault was John McCallum, who to his credit didn't lose his nerve, taking six wickets in a match the next day!

5. THE LAWS of cricket seemingly provide for everything and umpires really have to know them backwards. Usually umpires make the key decisions, such as when play should proceed or stop after rain or a storm. But in the Mornington Peninsula Cricket Association, it's the local *boatman* and not the umpire who decides!

How so? Well, Rule 37 of the MPCA reads: 'If the boatman considers the bay too rough on the second day of a two-day match with French Island, then the match is to be deemed a draw unless a decision was reached on the first day.'

French Island is in Westernport Bay, along with Phillip Island, of penguin rookery fame, and has always been a key member of the local cricket association, competing against teams based on the mainland — the Mornington Peninsula, south of Melbourne.

The French Island XI has always been big on hospitality and it's not unusual for visiting players to be so overcome by the hospitality that they don't return to the mainland until the Monday or Tuesday.

6. HOW ABOUT these unusual circumstances, where an A-grade semi-final match in the Jika and Preston District Cricket Association in Melbourne in the mid-1980s was abandoned…

Saturday's play between Northern Socials and Kingsbury was washed out and the men returned on the Sunday. About 10 overs had been bowled when a women's cricket team turned up and demanded that the blokes vacate the ground immediately so they could play their match.

The women reckoned their game was vital as it was to decide who played in the finals. The men told them that their game was also a semi-final and could they please get off the ground as fast as possible.

At first it seemed that the men's argument was stronger as the ladies started trooping off. But one powerfully-built woman was far from impressed. She stormed the pitch, cursing and yelling, removed the bails and hurled a stump an estimated 70 metres!

The men watched the stump sail over the head of fine leg, hastily convened a mid-pitch meeting and decided to beat an honourable retreat. Anyone who could throw a stump 70 metres had to be respected!

7. LOVE THIS little yarn about Edgar Emery, the 'Don Bradman of the South Coast', who made 75 centuries, including a highest of 314 for Gerringong against Shell Harbour in October 1938. According to my sources, Emery hit 27 sixes and 24 fours — 258 runs in boundaries.

The local newspaper reported: 'Edgar Emery must be the only cricketer in history to play a long innings with 10 fieldsmen on the oval and the 11th man fielding *outside* the boundary, in the paddock behind straight hit — by order of the captain. (His main task was to return the ball to the actual playing area, when Edgar's soaring hits frequently cleared the fence.)

'Round Toolijoa, Foxground and Crooked River way, the farmers used to hunt all their cows out of the paddocks surrounding the ground, on which the match against Emery's teams was to be played.'

8. THE DISTINCTION of having made the fastest century ever in Australia belongs to two men, both Queensland bush cricketers, one from Cairns and the other from Townsville. In February 1918, Cairns cricketer Laurie Quinlan took just 18 minutes to score 100 not out, for Trinity against Mercantile. He struck eight sixes and eight fours. Sixty-eight years later, Russell Penny also made 100 in 18 minutes during the 1985-86 Goldfield 'Ashes' series at Charters Towers.

9. AUSTRALIA'S 'MYSTERY' spinner John Gleeson once insured his right hand for $10,000 with insurance brokers Lloyds of London. Dubbed the 'Tamworth Twister', he was fascinated by the grip 1950s spinner Jack Iverson employed and gradually developed his control to such an extent that he ignored his batting/wicket-keeping roles to concentrate on bowling.

Gleeson's wiles fascinated the cricket world during the 1960s. Sir Don Bradman, then in his late 50s, asked for a private session in the nets with Gleeson.

Sir Donald was clad in civilian clothes and didn't worry about a bat. 'I tossed my off spinner high so it would take spin and he came across to let it go and it came back and hit him on the leg,' Gleeson said. Even the Don wasn't sure which way Gleeson's breaks were going.

10. THIS IS not just another tall Tangles tale which has developed on the sportman's night circuit over the years; it actually happened and the incident in question remains the highest number of runs scored from a single hit.

When a touring team from Victoria played a scratch XI from Bunbury in Western Australia, the opening ball of the match was hit into a three-pronged branch of a jarrah tree. The home side claimed 'lost ball' but the umpire ruled it was not lost as it could be seen. As the perplexed Sandgropers tried to figure out how to retrieve the missile, the Victorian openers continued to scamper up and down the wicket, piling on the runs!

The Bunbury boys sent for an axe but none could be found. Eventually, a rifle was produced and after numerous attempts, the ball was shot out of the tree, a little worse for wear! The Victorian score? 0 for 286! The visiting captain immediately declared, his side easily bowled out the opposition and everyone got into the refreshments early, with a real tall tale to tell!

The best centuries I've seen

WITH APOLOGIES to the Chappell brothers — who both played some marvellous century knocks for Australia — the most memorable hundreds of my time involved one man, Kevin Douglas Walters, the 'Dungog Dasher', a remarkable character and one of the foremost 'hard-wicket' batsmen of the modern era.

Three of Dougie's 100s stand out — his century between tea and stumps against England at Perth in 1974-75 and two on tours to New Zealand, the first at Auckland in 1973-74 and the second at Christchurch in 1976-77.

Hooking Bob Willis for six from the last delivery of the day to reach 103 not out was an incredible effort and very satisfying for Doug as he'd missed out against the Poms on the '72 tour.

The previous summer, his unbeaten 104 against the Kiwis, after coming in at 4 for 37 was a magician's knock. Eden Park that day was wet, underprepared and a seamer's paradise. Hardly any of us could get bat on ball, bar Doug who made 104 in 160 minutes, Chappelli (37 runs) and later Marshy (45). Eighteen wickets

100 up! Dougie Walters pulls Bob Willis for six to bring up his century between tea and stumps in the second Test, Perth, 1974-75.

fell on that opening day and the game was to finish in three days.

The highest of Doug's 15 Test centuries came three years later, again in New Zealand, this time at Christchurch. Thanks to Doug, we scored 552 after he'd come in at 4 for 112. The Kiwis had a good attack — the two Hadlee brothers, Ewen Chatfield and Hedley Howarth — but none had an answer to Doug's brilliance.

More than half his 250 runs came in boundaries and he struck the ball with such force that several times Kiwi fieldsmen preferred to let the ball go to the fence, rather than risk injury by stopping it. 'Gus' Gilmour also got a quick century and, with Doug, added a record 217 in just over three hours.

The gutsiest century I've seen came from Kim Hughes against the West Indies in the Christmas Test of 1981-82.

There's probably never been a more hostile pace attack than the Calypso quartet of Andy Roberts, Michael Holding, Joel Garner and Colin Croft — with apologies to Messrs Marshall, Ambrose, Walsh and Patterson — and on a greenish Melbourne wicket, the West Indians tore into their work. After just 50 minutes, Australia was 3 for 8, including skipper Greg Chappell first ball. Allan Border had batted an hour for four and Graeme Wood 50 minutes for three.

Batting at No. 5, Hughes was struck tremendous blows — on the ankle, on his fingers and on his right thigh. There hadn't been such fast bowling at the MCG since the days of Frank 'Typhoon' Tyson in 1954-55.

Holding was devastating, taking five wickets, one every three overs. Radar guns timed his deliveries at 85 m.p.h. Croft's fastest were 84 m.p.h. while Roberts averaged in the high 70s. It was one of those days where I was perfectly happy to be in the pavilion, involved purely as a commentator.

Hughes remained resolute, survived a confident lbw appeal at 13 and could have been caught at 24, but by the time Australia's last man, Terry Alderman, came in, Hughes was 71 and Australia 9 for 155.

No one had given a thought to the possibility of Hughes scoring a century. But with Alderman courageously hanging in — he was struck twice, on the arm

Kim Hughes is congratulated by West Indian skipper Clive Lloyd after his remarkable century in the Christmas Test, 1981-82.

by Croft and on the helmet by Garner — Hughes started to play with all his renowned aggression and scored 29 of a 43-run partnership.

He reached his 100 in 262 minutes with 11 fours. The Windies had been loath to applaud his 50 but were unanimous in their praise when he reached the ton.

Hughes's hands were jarred and battered and he had several big bruises as souvenirs, but it's doubtful if he ever played a more valuable knock for his country. It was a remarkable innings and I was privileged to be among the 30,046 Melburnians who saw it.

The best techniques I know

1. Batting

THERE'S NOTHING better than having someone throw the ball to you in the nets from just 10 paces away. Your footwork becomes all-important and you get the feel of bat regularly striking ball. You start hitting the ball in the sweet spot and it starts to fairly bound into the back of the net.

My Dad, Big Max, used to do it for hours with me. He'd nominate the shot he wanted me to play and would throw the appropriate ball. I'd play a dozen off-drives in a row, followed by 10 hooks and 10 cuts. By knowing what to expect, I was in position and, more often than not, would hit it in the middle of the bat. I could feel the confidence surging through me.

This technique really helps but I'm surprised how few of the good players actually do it on a regular basis. I reckon it's a must for every practice session, even if it's only for three or four minutes.

2. Bowling

BOWLING IS hard work and there's no substitute for practice but sometimes a few mid-match adjustments can make all the difference.

Fancy falling to this! Greigy tricks me with a slower one and I hole out, caught and bowled. I was looking good, too, and needed only another 83 for my maiden Test century!

Seam up and watch it wobble...you'd have to be a good batsman to play this one!

Keith 'Stacky' Stackpole would watch me like a hawk from first slip and if I wasn't hitting the seam, he'd bustle down to me between overs, asking if I was fair dinkum and whether I'd like to field fine leg at both ends of the ground! 'You're not hitting the seam, you big so-and-so,' Stacky would bleat. 'Let's see you charge through and get the seam up so it can swing and bounce a bit.'

We'd developed an exercise which helped me to bowl with the seam straight and at the start of an over, or at drinks, Stacky would get 10 paces from me and I'd throw five or six balls to him, making sure the seam was vertical. Invariably, the ball would bend in the air with the natural flow of the arm. Then I'd bowl one or two using the same grip, again with the seam vertical, and they'd swing too.

In 50 seconds, I'd regain the swing I'd been looking for. Making sure the ball left my hand correctly was the key.

The 'done' thing and why players should behave

TIMES HAVE advanced rapidly since my youth when we tuned our crystal sets into those crackly sound waves bounced from one side of the world to the other, telling us of the deeds of our Aussie cricket heroes in the England.

As kids growing up, there was no such thing as televised cricket, especially from overseas. The first ABC telecasts didn't occur until 1958-59 and even then only the final session was shown — and only to Melbourne and Sydney viewers. The pictures didn't get down as far as Hobart town!

We had to use our imaginations, and wonder at the elegance of a Peter May drive or the velocity at which 'Fiery' Freddie Trueman propelled the ball.

Today, the electronic age allows us to see the best — and the worst — of cricket, from most centres in the world. Unconsciously we are coached by the players — the slow-motion replays depicting every good shot or dismissal from three or four different angles.

We see the antics of the fast bowlers like Geoff Lawson and Dennis Lillee or the frustration of a dismissed batsman, like England's Chris Broad, who knocked down his stumps with his bat after making 139 in the Bicentennial Test in Sydney.

Sometimes players forget the huge responsibilities of being a Test player. Youngsters are so easily led. They mimic every movement of the stars. As 12- and 13-year-olds, we learnt to walk exactly like our heroes, copying every mannerism. The power of the small screen is so immense and many senior players are yet to realise their obligations to the spirit of the game. Umpires must show much commonsense to make sure that matters don't get out of hand.

Tennis bad-boy John McEnroe may complain at being fined a lot of money. He says officials are trying to force him to be robot-like. Unfortunately kids think his behaviour is the norm, when it's not acceptable in any shape or form.

The greatest team I ever played against

I WAS involved in the most exciting decade of cricket ever, the 1970s, when many of the elite, establishment cricketers joined Kerry Packer's World Series Cricket.

We were like cowboys in the wild west, parading in coloured gear, playing at night with white balls. Night-time cricket was virtually unheard of, yet we got the

Hooked on Cricket

grounds and took our cricket around Australia, to major cities as well as rural areas. It was an incredibly exciting two-year period, before a compromise was reached, and at the start of the 1979-80 summer, we returned to traditional ranks.

The WSC Australian team in those breakaway years was arguably the best XI in the world. The cricket we played was to an incredibly high standard, our opposition absolutely world class.

In the first season, 1977-78, the WSC Australians played 'Supertests' against the West Indies (losing 2-1), while the cream of the West Indians were involved in three 'Supertests' with the Rest of the World team against us. Again we lost 2-1. But the next year we beat the West Indies 1-0 and, on a tour of the Caribbean, tied the five-'Supertest' series 1-1.

When the elite players in the West Indian side were also involved in the WSC World XI, it was a truly magnificent side, by far the best cricket team I've ever competed against.

How's this for a combination (in batting order) — Barry Richards (South Africa), Gordon Greenidge (West Indies), Viv Richards (West Indies), Clive Lloyd

How's this for a line-up? Left to right (in batting order): Barry Richards (South Africa), Gordon Greenidge (West Indies), Viv Richards (West Indies), Clive Lloyd (West Indies), Asif Iqbal (Pakistan), Tony Greig (England), Imran Khan (Pakistan), Alan Knott (England), Wayne Daniel (West Indies), Andy Roberts (West Indies)) and Derek Underwood (England).

(West Indies), Asif Iqbal (Pakistan), Tony Greig (England), Imran Khan (Pakistan), Alan Knott (England), Wayne Daniel (West Indies), Andy Roberts (West Indies)) and Derek Underwood (England).

We played this team in the second 'Supertest' at Gloucester Park, Perth, in 1977-78 and, after a day and a bit, the Rest was 1 for 461. Openers Barry Richards (207) and Greenidge (140) added 369 for the first wicket. Then Viv Richards came in and rifled 177. They made 625 and despite 174 runs from Greg Chappell, we were beaten inside four days.

I won't forget that game in a hurry — I had 115 runs blasted from 14 overs and didn't take a wicket! We fought back in the final game to win by 41 runs at VFL Park, Greg Chappell making 246 not out, a marvellous effort.

In that first year of World Series Cricket, I got 26 wickets in the six 'Supertests'. Only one player, West Indian Andy Roberts, equalled that mark. His 26 cost him 21 runs apiece. Mine cost around 23. I got 7 for 88 in the fourth 'Supertest' of the summer at the Sydney Showgrounds and among them were some reasonably 'useful' names — Barry Richards, Viv Richards, Gordon Greenidge, Clive Lloyd, Mike Procter and Greigy — a particularly satisfying wicket!

Days like that make it all worthwhile. A fortnight later, I was being blasted to every corner of Gloucester Park. Funny game, cricket!

The most valuable lesson I ever learnt

IT WAS about life more than cricket. I was captain of the school under-14 team. My pal Johnny Neilson was vice-captain. The match against Hutchens School was just finishing when Johnny's Dad came up and said: 'How'd you go, Max?'

I said: 'I got 51 not out, Mr Neilson.'

'Don't ever let me hear that sort of reply again,' he said. 'When I asked you how did you go, I meant the team. Always put your team first, Max. If you're a good enough player, someone else will tell me how well you've done.'

I was really embarrassed. I learnt that day that you never need to sing your own song. I tell my boy, Tristan, that now. It helps to be a little humble, not self-centred. The biggest turn-off to me in the world is a big-headed sportsman, particularly one who can't play.

After that encounter with Johnny's Dad, I would hardly say a word! It was an attitude lesson which I adopted from that day on.

The truth about 'Chappelli' and the Coke bottle
(or how to make your cricket bat useful and ensure its long life)

THE BEST bowlers in the world aren't the ones who can swing the ball at right angles, cut it the most, or spin it prodigiously. They are generally the guys who are very, very quick at analysing the opposition.

Dennis Lillee was expert at 'reading' the faults of batsmen. It would take him only two or three deliveries and he'd be working at exploiting a weakness or two.

Bowlers should think deeply, not only when they are bowling but also when resting between overs. Is the batsman a front-foot or back-foot player? He may like the drive but is his foot always close to the ball? What about his stance — is there too much of a gap between the bat where it rests on the ground near his toes? The daylight in there can usually be exploited, with an off-break, in-dipper or off-cutter.

The same batsman may not pick up his bat straight, making it very difficult for him to 'flow' through the line of the ball. He might tend to hit towards the leg side all the time, making him suspect to the out-swinger.

A cricket bat is only four inches wide and the ball which deviates away will invariably find an edge and scoot into the slips.

Bowlers must have a plan for every batsman. They must ask themselves: 'How am I going to get this chap out? Will I get him caught in the slips? Perhaps he'll lob a catch to gully.'

Eighty per cent of the wickets taken in a cricket match fall to catches, so a bowler must have his field carefully placed, to suit the strengths — and weaknesses — of the player on strike. Batsmen may bemoan the fact that they're forever falling to incredible catches and just have no luck, but when they hit the ball in the air, that's the risk they take.

The bottom hand, which gives a player the power and the strength, is also the one which is going to get him out. If you play with your top hand and keep the handle of the bat in front of the ball at the point of contact, you can't hit the ball in the air. One way of making sure you don't 'scoop' the ball is by thickening the handle at the base with tape, or by cutting an extra rubber grip in half and working the two halves down to the lower section of the handle. It makes it impossible for you to hold the bat as tightly with the bottom hand.

Former Victorian captain Johnny Scholes hurt his hand during a big innings at Albert Ground in a Melbourne District final and couldn't hold his bat properly. They taped his bat handle enough to enable him to at least grip the bat and he relied on glides and deflections for his runs. All the power was generated from his top hand.

A bat often 'picks up' a lot better with extra grips. West Indian Clive Lloyd sometimes used five or six grips. Pick-up can be altered dramatically by changing the thickness of the handle. Lloyd liked flexibility with his bats, which weighed more than most but seemed like a matchstick in his huge hands.

Another Test skipper, Ian Chappell, also went for a flexible handle, but I can't say I recommend his technique. He'd get a Coke bottle and one of his brand-new, $180 double-scoop Gray-Nicolls bats, kneel on the splice and, using the bottle as the fulcrum, roll the bat back and forth so that the handle was nice and whippy. If he went too far and the handle broke, he'd just get another one. He could afford it; he endorsed them!

Other players like stiff handles which aren't as flexible. I wasn't as lucky as Chappelli and, especially in the early days, had to buy all my own bats. I'd really work on them, hardening the face, so they'd last that little bit longer.

I'd look for a bat which had a slight curve, make sure its weight suited me and 'picked up' nicely. I'd then get an old, much-loved, flattish bone and slide it up and down the face of the bat, compressing the fibres and toughening the blade.

An alternative was to roll the bat over the edge of a bath or a hand basin, pushing

Ian Chappell loved to take the attack to the bowling — with one of his 'whippy'-handled bats.

it up and down, using just enough linseed oil to keep the face of the bat moist and the particles compressed without fear of the blade drying or cracking.

Definitely do *not* put the bat's toe in a saucer of linseed oil! 'Rowdy' Mallett did this when he was a youngster and wondered why he couldn't pick up the bat afterwards! The blade swells and resembles a club, rather than a cricket bat. No wonder Rowd never used to make many against us!

Another 'no no' is for Mum or Dad to buy a $200 bat for junior and put it away for his birthday or Christmas. Even if it spoils that element of surprise, the youngster must have the opportunity of picking his own bat and have access to some expert advice while doing it.

Bats with pig skin around the middle or blades covered by 'long-lasting' material should also be avoided, as often the covering will hide defects in the bat.

My first bat was a hand-hammered, cashmere willow job and cost my Dad, Big Max, one pound 10 shillings. On the first day out, I tried to hammer in the stumps with the face, Big Max saw me and boy, did he pay out on me! 'Use the handle, use the handle!' were among some of the things he said; the others couldn't be repeated here! Then I had a Sir Leonard Hutton world-record five-crown bat which was a beauty, except I was only a little tyke and couldn't pick it up!

Many mature cricketers play with ultra-heavy bats, and wonder why they can't hook and cut like they used to! At coach Bobby Simpson's recommendation, most of the Australian players now use lighter bats. Top-rating pair David Boon and Dean Jones prefer their bats to weigh-in at under 2 pounds 7 ounces. Previously they used bats as heavy as 2 pounds 12 ounces.

The heavy bats gained popularity when Ian Botham and New Zealander Lance Cairns were at the height of their fame early in the 1980s. Some of 'Both's' Duncan Fearnley Magnums weighed as much as 3 pounds 6 ounces; Cairns's Newbery bats were even heavier.

The Chappell brothers and Rodney Marsh tended to go for heavier bats. I used 'Marshy's' bat once. I made only 21 but in the finish, my wrists and arms were aching so much I could hardly bowl.

Postwar batting greats like Simpson and Dougie Walters played with bats weighing 2 pounds 4 ounces and less — yet Dougie was one of the biggest hitters in the game. It gets back to how a player times the stroke. There aren't too many bat-makers around who make a nicely-balanced, lighter bat these days, but there's a market for them.

Youngsters should use bats which suit their height and strength. If a bat is too big, cut a bit off the bottom. To compensate for his height, Tony Greig had his bats specially made an inch and a half longer.

My most cherished bats included a five-star Neil Harvey one, which a family friend, Artie James, the masseur to many Australian cricket teams, brought back from England for me. Four years later, when I was 16, he gave me a Richie Benaud-autographed Gray-Nicolls and my first pair of pads, a pair of Jack Hobbs buckskins. They were rippers. The bat and pads lasted me right through to my first tour of the West Indies with the 1973 Australians.

We got to Bridgetown, Barbados, where I met a young boy called Joey, who grinned non-stop and always appeared to be around, wishing me well. He wasn't brash or cheeky like some of the other kids, but just a genuine nice little guy.

The game finished early due to rain and I got into a conversation with him outside the rooms. He was cricket-mad and knew all the statistics and played every day with his mates. Before the game I'd just got a new bat and pads from Gray-Nicolls and I said to Joey: 'Look, if I give you a pair of pads, do you reckon you could use them?'

I don't think I've ever seen anyone's eyes light up so much. 'Gee, Mr Walker, we ain't got no pads, we ain't got no bat, we ain't got nothing.' I gave him the pads, which were almost as big as he was, and off he went, proud as Punch, with about 40 kids straggling along behind him. I bet little Joey still treasures those pads, even if he has grown a little!

Twisters from Tangles
- Turn to pages 93-95 for Twister answers.

1. Anagrams:
UNRAVEL THESE mystery combinations and find the surnames of six Australian Test cricketers:
1. MAD BARN
2. LOCK PASTE
3. DANUBE
4. LOU GRIM
5. RED ROB
6. WET MATHS

'Gus' Gilmour: an incredible talent and gifted, left-arm swing bowler.

2. Nicknames:
WHICH RECENT Australian cricketers carried these nicknames?

1. 'Rowdy'
2. 'Roo'
3. 'Phantom'
4. 'The Griz'
5. 'Spotty'
6. 'Bertie'
7. 'Stumpy'
8. 'Garth'
9. 'Wocka'
10. 'Bish'
11. 'Claggie'
12. 'Cho' (Cricket Hours Only)
13. 'Slippery'
14. 'Jake the Peg'
15. 'Jaffa'

3. True or false?
1. Kerry O'Keeffe opened the batting for Australia.
2. Jeff Thomson captained Australia.
3. Ian Chappell, Graham Yallop and Allan Border all kept wickets for Australia.
4. In the Australia—England Christmas Test of 1982-83, Australian batsmen ignored the opportunity of running almost 30 comfortable singles and lost by three runs.
5. I captained Australia.
6. New South Wales teams of the '50s fielded total Test XIs.
7. Tasmania's first Test cricketer was David Boon.
8. Rod Marsh bowled for Australia.

9. Paul 'Dasher' Hibbert, the former Victorian and Australian opener, earned his nickname through his inspired, attack-at-all-times strokeplay.
10. Sir Garfield Sobers, Barry Richards, Younis Ahmed and Lance Gibbs all played for South Australia.

4. For the buffs

1. Who was best man at Jeff Thomson's wedding?
2. Which famous Australian cricketer was named after two aviators?
3. Who called his autobiography *Run Digger*?
4. Which South Australian import was sponsored at $1 a run during the 1970-71 season?
5. For which English county teams did these Aussies play?: (a) Ian Chappell; (b) Geoff Lawson; (c) Allan Border; (d) Jeff Thomson; (e) Denis Hickey; (f) Rod McCurdy; (g) Alan Connolly.
6. Which Australian father and son played for Somerset?
7. Who was the Australian batsman run out to force Test cricket's first tie?
8. Don Bradman was dismissed for a duck only seven times in Test cricket. Who were the bowlers?
9. Which Australian player broke his ankle while bowling leg breaks in the 1938 Test matches?
10. What was the new nickname given to Wayne Phillips after he had compiled a brilliant 120, batting at No. 8 against world champions West Indies at Bridgetown in 1984?
11. Name the only Australian to play World Series Cricket, Test cricket and with Kim Hughes's 'rebels' in South Africa.
12. In what Test match of the 1980s did five left-handed batsmen fill the top six places in the Australian batting line-up? Name the players.
13. Who were the Dunce brothers?
14. Who batted for 250 minutes for 28 not out (an average of seven runs an hour) for Australia against England in Brisbane's 'Battle of the Snooze' in 1958-59?
15. Which teenage bowler was invited to the Adelaide nets as a net bowler for the 1960-61 West Indians and bowled four batsmen — skipper Frank Worrell, Gary Sobers, Rohan Kanhai and Conrad Hunte? Hint: Four years later he played for Australia.

5. Did you know?

- KIM HUGHES is the only Australian to bat on every day of a five-day Test match. He scored 117 and 84 during the 1980 Centenary Test at Lord's.
- My skinny mate Ian Redpath once hit 32 runs (6 6 6 6 4 4) off a six-ball over. The unlucky bowler was South African Neil Rosendorff in the Australians versus Orange Free State game at Bloemfontein in 1969-70.
- Bodyline bowler Harold Larwood struck Australian batsmen 34 times during his 15 Tests. Bill Woodfull, Bill Ponsford and Jack Fingleton were his most frequent victims.
- The great Greg Chappell scored seven ducks, including four in a row, against Pakistan and the West Indies during the 1981-82 season. It was a most

remarkable run of outs, which pleased only a few — Chappell's opponents and cartoonists Australia-wide.
- Australia's first Prime Minister, Edmund Barton, was also an umpire during his younger years. Among the fixtures he officiated at was the controversial NSW–England game of 1878-79 when a run-out decision by fellow umpire George Coulthard sparked a riot.
- The only Australian to be given out 'handled ball' in a Test is Andrew Hilditch, against Pakistan in Perth in 1979.
- The 'in-house' nickname given to Greg Chappell by his teammates was 'God' — for his dignified manner and the miracles he performed with the bat.

6. *Successful partnerships*

COMPLETE THE missing names of these successful Australian partnerships:
(a) Miller and — (8 letters)
(b) Boon and — (5)
(c) Thomson and — (6)
(d) Loxton, Seddon and — (7)
(e) Lawry and — (7)

Anagram answers: 1. Bradman; 2. Stackpole; 3. Benaud; 4. Gilmour; 5. Border; 6. Matthews.

Nickname answers: 1. Ashley Mallett; 2. Bruce Yardley; 3. Bill Lawry; 4. Wally Grout; 5. Ray Bright; 6. Ian Chappell; 7. Bruce Laird; 8. Graham McKenzie; 9. John Watkins; 10. Rick McCosker; 11. Kim Hughes; 12. John Gleeson; 13. Lenny Pascoe; 14. Gary Gilmour; 15. Gary Cosier.

True or false answers:
1. True. Skully opened the second innings of the Centenary Test when Rick McCosker had a broken jaw. He made 14 and with Ian Davis added 33 for the first wicket.
2. True. Thommo was vice-captain to Bobby Simpson on the 1978 West Indian tour and captained at Antigua in between Test matches. Legend has it that he told his players at the start: 'I'm bowling, spread out!'
3. True. Yallop even took a catch, when deputising for John Maclean in the fourth Test of 1978-79. He caught Ian Botham off the bowling of Rodney Hogg.
4. True. Allan Border and Jeff Thomson added 70 runs in more than two hours for the final wicket. Border, in his attempts to 'farm' the strike, often preferred to remain at the batting end instead of taking singles which would have seen No. 11 player Thomson on strike. It was an incredibly exciting finish, England scoring 284 and 294, Australia 287 and 288.
5. False. I would have loved to, but the powers-that-be usually reserve such responsibility for batsmen. I reckon I would have made a good, consistent skipper — I would have bowled from one end all day, and allowed the rest to squabble over the other end!
6. Almost true. The odd man out was wicket-keeper Dougie Ford who didn't play

Test cricket; the rest did! No wonder they won 10 Sheffield Shields in 11 years.
7. False. He was the first Test man to be produced from Shield ranks, but before him, Tasmanian Test cricketers included 'Jack' Badcock, Laurie Nash, Charlie Eady and Ken Burn.
8. True. And Bacchus is proud of it, too. It happened at Faisalabad during the three-Test Australian tour of Pakistan. In a rain-affected game, Australia scored 617 and Pakistan replied with 2 for 382. Skipper Greg Chappell kept wicket after tea on the final day, allowing Marshy to have 10 overs, 0 for 51. It had been 100 years since all 11 players had bowled in a Test innings.
9. False. Dash liked to take his time and is famous for being the only Australian I can remember who has ever made a century *without* scoring a four! His monumental century for Victoria against India in November 1977 took 327 minutes, but earned him his one and only Test match later that summer.
10. True. Sobers and Richards were particularly successful, Sobers being the only player to score 1000 runs and take 50 wickets in an Australian first-class season (1962-63 and 1963-64) while Richards is famous for scoring 356 for South Australia against Western Australia including 325 in a day in 1970-71. Younis Ahmed and Lance Gibbs both played Shield cricket for South Australia for one season.

---

7. Blind man's cricket

THIS IS a more sophisticated version of the game I sometimes played during physics classes at school. I used a special pencil on which I'd carved 'one, two, three, four, no ball and wicket' on its six facets. I call it 'Blind man's cricket' and here are the basic rules:

1. Create your own scoring diagram using the one below as a general guide. Any size will do. If you have use of a photocopier, you can make several copies. For party games, make a larger version and pin it to a board. You can make the game more difficult by marking more 'outs' than shown here, or easier by having more 'runs' squares.
2. You can have any number of players, from two to 22, plus two umpires and two scorers to create a match atmosphere.
3. Toss to see who bats or bowls first. The 'batsman' closes his or her eyes (or you can use a blindfold), the 'bowler' spins the scoring diagram, so the batsman cannot remember the positions, and calls 'Play'.
4. The batsman then stabs a finger or pencil down on the diagram (fond fathers and mothers can make miniature cricket bats to be used as pointers for young players) and either registers runs or outs.
5. The umpires judge whether the 'bat' is on a line or in a square; the scorers keep a record of the game, of course.
6. You can set a time limit and captains can also make declarations. Of course, the weather will not interfere with play but you might like to mark 'Rain stops play' or 'Bad light' to provide a break.

For the buffs answers: 1. Greg Chappell; 2. Keith Ross Miller (after aviators Keith and Ross Smith); 3. Bill Lawry; 4. Barry Richards, from South Africa; 5. (a) Lancashire; (b) Lancashire; (c) Gloucestershire and Essex; (d) Middlesex; (e) Glamorgan; (f) Derbyshire; (g) Middlesex; 6. Colin and Russell McCool; 7. Ian Meckiff; 8. In order: H. C. Griffith (West Indies), W. E. Bowes, G. O. B. Allen, W. Voce, A. V. Bedser, A. V. Bedser, W. E. Hollies (all England); 9. Don Bradman. His foot was caught in a worn foothole and he was carried off. He couldn't bat in the match and Australia lost by an innings and 579 runs, the biggest defeat ever; 10. Spaceman; 11. Graham McKenzie; 12. In Australia's inaugural Test versus Sri Lanka in 1982-83. The 'top six' batting order was: Wessels, Wood, Yallop, G. Chappell, Hookes and Border; 13. 'Bertie' Chappell, 'Freddie' Walters and 'Herbie' Taber; 14. Jim Burke; 15. David Sincock.

Your rating: Questions correct: 1-8: Good. 9-14: Excellent. All 15: You must have peeked at the answers!

Successful partnerships answers: (a) Lindwall; (b) Marsh; (c) Lillee; (d) Bradman; (e) Simpson.

'Blind man's' cricket match board

OUT BOWLED	SCORE 6	OUT L.B.W.	SCORE 4	OUT OBSTRUCTION
OVER-THROW SCORE 1	OUT CAUGHT	SCORE 3	OUT HANDLED BALL	SCORE 5
OUT HIT WICKET	SCORE 2	RETIRED HURT	OUT CAUGHT	0
SCORE 6	APPEAL but NOT OUT	SCORE 1	OUT STUMPED	LEG BYE
WIDE	SCORE 1	OUT BOWLED	SCORE 4	NO BALL

You can pass away a few hours with 'Blind man's cricket'. Keep a scorebook next to you, name two 'best of' teams and score as you go.

Ugly scenes at the MCG and other commentary classics

I MADE an unforgettable entry into the world of commentary at the Melbourne Cricket Ground. It was a one-day international and it was hot — steaming hot. The forecast was for 40 degrees but I still lobbed in my best bag of fruit, cut lunch under my arm, ready for anything. It was the first time I'd ever worked with Alan McGilvray. It was a real red-letter day.

At the time, the ABC broadcast from these quaint, old boxes in the middle of the cigar stand in the Melbourne Cricket Club Members. I reckon the boxes were built around Governor Macquarie's day and were ideal for two dwarfs, but not for a scorer and two commentators — one of whom was a former footballer who had added a few pounds since retirement. There was no such thing as air-conditioning and I reckon it must have been 45 degrees inside. You could have fried eggs in there.

I was taking over from Norman O'Neill who had the first shift and to get into position, I had to clamber over Alan 'Mac' McGilvray. Mac had his binoculars up and was on air, talking about the action. As I came over the top, in my eagerness to get into my possie, I kneed him in the back of the head and nearly put him and his binoculars through the front panel of glass.

Mac somehow retained his composure and apologised to me, but I assured him my size 14s were at fault. Then, after getting passed Mac, I upset scorer Jack Cameron's pride-and-joy, his black box of cards which contained all the scores and stats you'd need to talk through any rain-ruined Test match.

Jack's beautifully-kept cards had fallen out of the box and were scattered all over this tiny floor. Meanwhile, the game's still going on — there are no ads on the ABC — and Mac is doing his best to keep the commentary going; I'm scrambling for Jack's cards, Jack's scrambling for Jack's cards. Talk about a mess!

Alan McGilvray, doyen of Australian cricket commentators.

In the MCG commentary box with ABC broadcaster 'Smokey' Dawson. If you ever get to commentate with him, don't take any sponge cake with you!

I was beetroot red with embarrassment, my shirt was saturated in sweat and I hadn't even said a word!

I came out after my 40-minute segment, with my tie at mid-ships, suit jacket over my arm and shirt sleeves flapping. It was like a sauna, ideal for losing some weight, but not much fun on your first day of a new job.

Both Jack and Mac are great mates of mine but I still get embarrassed thinking about my inglorious beginning.

The ABC boys are a lot of fun and don't mind setting up a newcomer. Graham 'Smokey' Dawson shared sponge cake with Paul Sheahan at Geelong one day, and then threw a question to Paul just as he was putting a huge piece into his mouth! Chocky cake went everywhere as Paul did his best to reply, succeeding only in spraying the whole box with cake crumbs!

At Adelaide one day, we'd been given a big box of Mars bars and I was on-air with Jimmy Maxwell. At a news break, Jim reached for one and was unwrapping it like a banana when suddenly the 'standby' signal came through. Handing me the Mars bar he said: 'Take this; you'll have a couple of minutes before you're on. Go for it.' West Indian fast bowler Michael Holding had just started a new over and Jim's Mars bar looked pretty inviting. I did a quick calculation: I had a good four or five munching minutes to sit back and really enjoy myself.

In mid-over, Jim noticed my enjoyment and suddenly, out of the blue, threw an on-air question at me. Holding was at the head of his mark and Jim, with a wicked grin on his face, asked: 'Tangles, why don't you take us through this magnificent run up of Holding's. It really is poetry in motion, don't you think?'

Jim's timing was spot-on. I'd just taken a huge, last bite of this sticky chocolate bar. I tried to do as I was told, but instead of saying the right things all I could do was gurgle and splutter. Jim just sat back laughing and explained to ABC listeners Australia-wide that the 'big fella was hungry today and couldn't wait till lunchtime!'

About 20 minutes later — it took me that long to recover my composure — I was commentating and through my headphones heard this persistent 'click, click, click' sound. I did my best to keep going, wanting to let the technical guys know we had a strange noise coming through the headphones but there was no one around. I looked to Jim for guidance. Having just devoured one of the Mars bars himself, there he was trying to get the stickier parts off the roof of his mouth! I couldn't believe it. I was sure these 'click, click, click' sounds were going around the country, but Jimmy had turned off his mike — Maxwell 2, Walker 0.

I haven't been able to even the score as I've been with Channel Nine's *Wide World of Sports* team since then. It's been quite an education and since the Mars bar incident, I've made a golden rule not to eat while in the commentary box!

During the 1987-88 season in Perth, I was doing a stint with Tony Greig on radio 2UE and Greigy was talking when this huge fly flew straight into my mouth and down my throat — without touching the sides. It must have been a huge blowie. I didn't even have time to hit the cough button before breaking into massive wheezing and spluttering. Greigy turned around and said incredulously: 'What is going on here; are you all right?'

I mumbled something about how the fly was still walking down my throat, that it was a real Billy Bunter and could Greigy please continue without me. There

Richie Benaud (left) with another fairly well-known face, Prime Minister Bob Hawke, at Canberra's Manuka Oval, Prime Minister's XI versus West Indies, January 1985.

were tears rolling down my cheeks as the ghastly sounds of my coughs and splutters went out all over Sydney and suburbs, much to Greigy's amusement. He likes seeing Aussies in distress.

All the commentary boys have great fun, with lively banter back and forth, especially when a South Australian (Ian Chappell) is on with a Victorian (Bill Lawry).

Our chief cricket commentator, Richie Benaud, is renowned for his unflappable approach. He has a terrific, three-level briefcase, a swish, imported Italian job with brass edges and compartments for everything. Richie stacks a lot of things in there, from computers, batteries and tape recorders to copies of *Wisden* and other info. It weighs a ton and better Richie carry it than any of us.

We'd arrived at Adelaide's Footy Park for the first game of the 1987-88 season, a McDonald's Cup one-dayer, and hopping out of the car we were almost blown away by the wind. It was blowing a real gale. They'd just rigged up this little commentary box right at the top of the stand, about five storeys up. To get to it we had to shimmy up five sets of near-vertical steps. It was quite an effort.

Richie had his huge briefcase in one hand and was doing his best to clamber up. But the wind was very strong and he'd stopped just four steps up on the first tier when a huge gust made him miss his footing. There he was, blowing around in mid-air, grasping the stairs with one hand, his precious briefcase with the other.

He couldn't do a thing but hang on for dear life and limb. It was quite comical, really. His white hair, usually beautifully combed and presented, was standing up at attention and his tie and coat were flapping wildly in the wind. He didn't want to drop his bag and ruin all his electronic, whizz-bang things he had so carefully packed the night before. But the wind was howling and he was fast running out of options.

Richie must have been dangling from those stairs for a good 30 seconds before one of our 'gophers' — a youngster who was helping — saw what was happening and, clambering up the stairs, yelled to Richie: 'I'll take your bag, let go.'

Now Richie doesn't often smile on television, but boy was he grateful to this little fella. 'You sure can, son, you sure can. Thanks so much,' he said, breaking into this huge, cheesecake grin.

We were all watching this from the safety of the ground, believing that Richie, as a our leader, should test the stairs first and lead from the front. He eventually got up there safely, so did his bag. The rest of us followed, still smiling. It sure was a rickety little box — the wind appeared twice as strong five storeys up — but to make matters worse, there was no urn for a cup of coffee.

Richie's young saviour was still on hand and volunteered to return to ground level and bring back six coffees. We spotted him soon after, our coffees nicely balanced in a little cardboard pack, but halfway up the stairs, a huge gust hit him, picked up the tray and coffees and whooshed them straight out of his hand.

Talk about action! We reckoned there was as much action off the field as on during that cold, windy, Adelaide day.

Unforgettable moments

NO ONE will ever forget Rick McCosker's courageous stand at the Centenary Test in Melbourne in 1977. He must have walked under a ladder or knocked a

'The hair on the back of my neck stood up. No one in the rooms spoke as a dozen pair of eyes watched Rick walk to the wicket.' Australian opener Rick McCosker marches to the crease less than 48 hours after copping a bouncer in the face, 1977 Centenary Test versus England.

black cat over on the way to the game, for not only did he suffer a broken jaw after being hit in the face, he was also given out bowled as the ball rebounded onto his stumps.

It would have been easy and quite understandable for Rick to hide in his shell and not bat again. But he did, for his sake and for his country's cricketing pride.

With Australia trying to build a match-winning lead for England to chase on the last days, McCosker donned his gear and went out to bat again at No. 10 in our second dig. It was a marvellous, emotional moment when he emerged unannounced from the pavilion, his face swathed in bandages.

On his head was his Australian cap and I thought it was the only thing holding him together. The huge, grey-concrete colosseum erupted when the patrons saw who it was. They sang 'Waltzing McCosker, Waltzing McCosker'. It was an unforgettable moment.

Against doctor's orders, he'd gone back out there, in the cauldron of a Test match, the Centenary clash between cricket's greatest rivals.

The hair on the back of my neck stood up. No one in the rooms spoke as a dozen pairs of eyes watched Rick walk to the wicket. It must have been terribly difficult for him to mentally suppress the image of the gold Kookaburra which had crashed into his face barely 48 hours before.

But this kind of 'test' is one which separates the elite sportsman from the mere mortal. Rick made only a couple of dozen but the 50-odd partnership with Marshy set up the victory and we won the game. Seeing Rick go back and do it again will always remain a marvellous moment for me and the huge MCG crowd.

Australian sporting annals are littered with epic stories of courage. Dennis Lillee would play despite all sorts of pain. His philosophy was that if you were fit enough to walk through the gate, you were fit enough to play. There were times when he went on with hamstrings injuries strapped up, severe bouts of influenza, or loads of pain-killing pills jumping around inside him. He never made an excuse; he always gave it his best.

His inspirational example enabled our Australian teams of the 1970s to remain among the strongest combinations fielded since the days of Bradman.

Veletta and some fielding theory

AUSTRALIA HAS been blessed with some wonderful fieldsmen in my immediate memory. Champion batsmen like Neil Harvey and Norman O'Neill were marvellous fielders. Paul Sheahan was also excellent with an enormous throwing capability while Ross Edwards's athleticism at cover saved many runs in the mid-1970s when we had a devastating all-round team — dynamic leadership from the Chappell brothers and enormous batting, bowling and fielding reserves.

The slips catching of players like Ian and Greg Chappell, Dougie Walters — when he was used there — and Ashley Mallett in the gully was an enormous fillip for the bowlers. These guys all had phenomenal reflexes. I used to gaze in wonderment from my specialist deep fine leg possie as our close-in guys made a habit of taking even the half-chances.

Expert fielding has become even more of a necessity with the regular scheduling of one-day internationals. The quality of catching appears to have lifted considerably with players possessing greater fitness and flexibility.

The current Australian side is well served with some experts like Allan Border, a very safe slipsman who doubles as a mid-wicket fielder in the one-dayers; Geoff Marsh, either in the gully or short leg; and Dean Jones, a great outrider.

Probably the most versatile and exciting of all our fieldsmen is Western Australia's Michael Veletta, an enthusiastic young cricketer who has worked tirelessly to improve all departments of his game.

A breakthrough for Veletta came during the winter of 1985-86 when he stepped up his off-season fielding routines. Under the expert guidance Don Weir, a former Australian baseballer and Melbourne District cricketer, Veletta completely changed his fielding technique through hours of practice. Weir has rarely seen anyone as keen to improve who so readily put in the time to lift his standard.

Weir made Veletta concentrate on the rudiments of fielding and throwing. Between them they analysed the baseball fielding skills which could be successfully adapted to cricket. Veletta eliminated all unnecessary movement in his search for the fastest ways of returning the ball He developed skills while throwing from a crouched position, while he was off balance, and on the run.

His skills are particularly valuable when fielding within 30 or 40 metres of a batsmen looking to steal a short run. Saving time in gathering and throwing has helped Veletta to initiate run-outs even he would not have considered possible years ago. Veletta adopted part of the fielding program in his initial warm-up. He sits on the turf, flexing the muscles of his upper body, working on developing strength and flexibility in his torso and throwing arm.

From a crouched position he throws to targets 20 and 30 metres away, gradually progressing to standing throws. Refining his fielding skills has added another dimension to his cricketing wares. It's taken a lot of time but those who have seen some of his work, both close to the wicket and in his boundary patrolling of late, are in no doubt that Veletta is reaching a comparable standard to some of the best-known and most highly-rated fielders in Australian postwar cricket.

Mike Veletta starts with the basics: he's nice and relaxed and, with his elbow restricted, cocks his wrist ready to throw.

The side-on shot emphasises the importance of the cocked wrist.

No elbow movement, but he's thrown it 20 metres. You feel how important it is to whip the wrist through.

The side-on view: Mike's wrist extends itself at the opposite end of the arc, too.

Now he can get a bit more shoulder into it —again, concentrating on the wrist, but with a bit of shoulder 'rock' too.

Mike's follow-through, in the direction of the target, still with elbow restricted and arm locked.

Mike throws with his right arm and always tries to pick up on his right side. His body is crouched, ensuring a low centre of gravity and bringing his line of sight almost in behind the ball.

Mike prepares to throw from a crouched position. He brings the ball up from the centre of his body.

Mike's right arm assists in balance as he lines up the target.

Still in a crouched position, Mike prepares to release. Notice the cocked wrist.

A front-on shot, a split second before the throw.

The release: Mike's thrown the ball almost 35 metres, still from a crouched position, using his upper body, arms and wrist to maximum effect.

Mike tries the drill standing up. It's a bit more comfortable, more natural. His elbow and wrist are cocked. His "support" arm aims at the target.

Mike takes one step towards his target and gathers to throw.

He completes the throw, his arm following through in the direction of the target, his left leg helping to retain balance.

An invaluable time-saving skill in getting to the ball and returning it with the least possible delay occurs by employing the 'cross-over' step. Mike's left leg comes across the body at full pace, allowing him to be in a virtual throwing position on running down the ball.

He gathers on the left foot, so he's immediately in a position to throw. This eliminates the extra step many take to balance themselves before throwing.

His 'trailing' leg splays around to provide Mike with the balance he needs to complete an accurate 50-metre throw.

Mike releases as quickly as possible, before taking another step. His throwing arm reaches for the target, eyes aimed firmly on the spot he wants to reach.

Gathering on the opposite side of the body, Mike is ready to swing around, again with the minimum of time wastage to allow him to make a good, fast, accurate return.

Wxyz

Watch and win

SO YOU are your team's all-rounder and won't be coming in until No. 7. You've got two hours to sit and relax and enjoy watching your mates get into the bowling.

Stay involved in the battle. If it's good enough for your teammates to be batting, it's good enough for you to watch. Try to assess who the best and most athletic fielders are. Who throws left-handed? Who throws with the right?

Make a mental note who not to take a short single to or, conversely, who appears to be slow and has a weaker arm. Imagine also where you would score most of your runs against a particular bowler.

If you're a bowler, work out where the breeze is coming from. Determine which end would suit you best. Talk to your captain about the opposition; try and pick up some info about their best bats. Analyse and discuss. Share your theories and bounce ideas around the room. It leads to a closer-knit and more successful team.

What's wrong with competing?

WHILE CRICKET is fun, it isn't the most essential part of the game for me. I disagree with those who claim that enjoyment should be rated ahead of trying to maximise one's potential through hours of practice and competition.

Some parents say I shouldn't teach kids to be so competitive. But why? There's nothing wrong with competing. Sure there's pressure, but what's wrong with that? As long as the lad can cope, that's fine.

From the moment of birth, we're competing — for fresh air, for Mum and Dad's attention, even for the use of our bat ahead of big brother who might also happen to fancy it. We compete at school, for chalk, teacher and friends. When we leave school, we are forced to compete, otherwise we don't get a job. Why take competition out of the classroom or schoolyard? Why not compete and compete well?

It's nice to play some games which are a little different, for example, rotation cricket and triangular cricket, but competition is what it's about.

Kids like competing and should be encouraged all the way. Dad not only must drive junior everywhere, he must also regularly get up on the roof and ferret out all the old tennis balls from the guttering and downpipes.

When former Australian one-day bowler Simon Davis shifted house as a youngster, his father, Frank, found 14 balls stuck in the downpipes. While some were 'unplayable', there were enough good 'uns to see young Simon through another season of backyard Test matches.

Next to his first bat and his autograph book, a cricket buff's best friend is a tennis ball. The best way a youngster can play cricket is with a tennis ball. It won't hurt him and will bounce evenly. You can hit across the line, playing the exciting leg-side shots, without the risk of getting hurt.

Youngsters may want to play with the big kids with a 'compo' ball but if they can

While most bowlers would prefer eight balls in an over, Glamorgan's Malcolm Nash was relieved he only had to bowl six, when West Indian Sir Garfield Sobers (pictured) struck six consecutive sixes, 36 runs in an over, playing for Nottinghamshire in an English county game at Swansea in 1968.

hang back and play with a tennis ball, they'll be better off in the long run. A tennis ball teaches hand-eye co-ordination.

However, they do have a habit of disappearing, over the fence or onto the roof. The trick is to live near a tennis court surrounded with shrubs! You're sure to find an ample supply every Monday after the weekenders have had their game.

Whoops, I've broken a window!

EVERY YOUNG cricketer worth his salt knows what it's like to break a window. You get that 'Oh no' sensation as the ball heads towards its target and a sinking feeling as it shatters the glass.

Some Dads hand out six-of-the-best and tell junior to hit the ball along the ground. They've 'been there and done that', too. The less fortunate have their bats confiscated for a week — that's agony!

We had a succession of accidents at the Old Empire Hotel where I was brought up. It was lucky for me that the glazier used to drink there most nights and gave Dad a discount.

But I did feel a whole lot better after I bowled one particular delivery to my Dad in the backyard of the old Empire. It hit a crack, one of those expansion joints in the concrete, and lifted dramatically. Dad's foot wasn't quite to the pitch of the ball for the intended flowing drive and the ball flew high over cover point, shattered the kitchen window and ended up in our old stainless steel sink!

'Didn't know you could bowl a leg cutter,' muttered Dad, going to survey the damage!

Why eight-ball overs are a must

CRICKET HAS always been set up to suit batsmen, and one of the strangest rule changes came in the reconciliation year between the Australian Cricket Board and Kerry Packer's World Series Cricket organisation.

In yet another slap at the bowlers, the authorities ruled that for the first time since the 'bodyline' season, six-ball overs would be reintroduced.

I'd grown up with eight-ball overs, believing the Australian way to be a fairer system than the six-ball regime which had for so long reigned in England. Getting all Test-playing countries to bowl six-ball overs makes sense but from a bowler's point of view, having only six in which to implement a plan is insufficient.

It's fine if you are going to blast out your opponent on a greenish deck where every delivery is a realistic wicket-taker. But spin bowlers and medium-pacers often take two or three overs to set up a strategy and the 'extra' two deliveries are absolutely invaluable.

Part of bowling strategy is to deny the 'on-strike' batsman one or two of his favourite shots and hope to force a mistake. If you can bowl two or three maidens in a row, and your opponent is still to get off the mark, he feels extra pressure.

Your captain can help by bringing in another close-in fielder, perhaps at silly mid-off, directly in eyeball range of the batter. That's when you might try one which is a fraction wider, a fraction slower and hope it swings slightly away.

The batsman is keen to 'move' the fielder who has come in short and in his eagerness, instead of having his foot correctly to the pitch of the ball, he tends to flay from the shoulders and manages to edge it into the gully. You've got him!

Having only six balls an over can be very frustrating as it's easier for a batsman to nick a single and scuttle to the safety of the non-striker's crease. It often means you have to wait another over, perhaps two, to get another go at him.

With eight-ball overs, a batsman may, for example, play and miss at your first and second and be hit on the pads by the next three. But instead of having to play only one more delivery for the 'safety' of the non-striker's end, he's still got three deliveries to survive. Mentally this doubles the pressure.

It's a hard enough game for bowlers now and if I had a vote at Australian Cricket Board level, I'd certainly bring back eight-ball overs. The Englishmen have generally played six balls an over but we didn't have to follow them.

The great majority of bowlers don't mind having an extra couple of deliveries up their sleeves. It makes for a more absorbing contest, and potentially could be terrific for the crowds who love to see a lot of runs off each over.

XXXX cricket
(or, the most amazing batting collapse I've seen)

Pakistan v Australia (first Test, 14 November 1981, WACA Ground, Perth)

Pakistan: First innings (started 11.55 a.m.)

11.57 a.m.
Mudassar, 0
Pakistan 1-1

12.01 p.m.
Rizwan, 0
Pakistan 2-1

12.19 p.m.
Miandad, 6
Pakistan 3-14

12.21 p.m.
Majid, 3
Pakistan 4-17

12.27 p.m.
Wasim Raja, 4
Pakistan 5-21

12.38 p.m.
Imran Khan, 4
Pakistan 6-25

12.51 p.m.
Mansoor, 6
Pakistan 7-25

Lunch: 1 to 1.40 p.m.

1.43 p.m.
Wasim Bari, 1
Pakistan 8-26

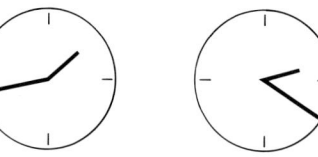

2.20 p.m.
Qasim Omar, 5
Pakistan 9-57

2.45 p.m.
Sarfraz, 26
Pakistan 10-62

Sikander was not out 3. The innings finished at 2.45 p.m. (Batting time: 108 minutes, overs: 21.3) Match scores: Pakistan 62 and 256. Australia 180 and 8 for 424 declared. Australia won by 286 runs.

ELSEWHERE AMONG these tales, I've talked about batting collapses and how there can be a real 'snowball' effect if a side loses early wickets and the middle-order batsmen fail to make a stand.

The 1981-82 touring Pakistanis suffered the ignominy of being bowled out for just 62 on the Saturday's play of the first Test.

It was an amazing sequence of events. Ten wickets fell for just 46 runs in the first session, after the Australians — resuming at 7 for 159 — were all out for 180. At lunch, Pakistan in reply was 7 for 25, Dennis Lillee having 4 for 14 and Terry Alderman 3 for 9, in his first Test at the WACA Ground.

Big Sarfraz Nawaz enlivened proceedings after lunch but the tourists still fell far short of their previous worst-ever score, 87 against England in 1954. While the wicket was greenish and the ball moved around considerably, it wasn't a bad wicket as the heavy scoring on the final three days showed.

Mudassar, Miandad and Majid Khan were all out to forgettable shots. Australian skipper Greg Chappell didn't even have to call on Thommo until the 19th over of the innings when Dennis took a rest, having taken 5 for 18 from nine overs!

Later in this game, Dennis Lillee was involved in the infamous 'toe-tapping/bat-waving' incident with Pakistani skipper Javed Miandad. He was to be fined $200.

Dennis Lillee and Pakistani captain Javed Miandad clash during the first Test of 1981 in Perth. If I was a little bloke like Javed, I'd want to carry a big stick when tackling Lillee, too!

You can't score runs sitting in the pavilion

WHEN YOU'RE at the crease, always remember that you're just one ball away from being dismissed; the very next ball could 'do' you.

You must guard against getting out, so you're there when the bad bowling comes. Then you can judge where to hit that bad ball, and how many you're looking to score, whether it be one, two, three or four.

I'm taking it for granted that you look like a cricketer, with immaculate gear, shoes nice and white, the buckles of your pads tucked in and not trailing.

When getting onto the front foot, you should try and 'tread' on the ball. If it takes two steps to do it, go for it. You're always going to be able to play better shots — more correctly and with less risk — when your foot is to the pitch of the ball. If you can't get to the pitch, then go back.

Cricket is a side-on game. You throw side-on, you bat side-on, you bowl side-on. The moment you square up, you're gone.

Youngsters should work on having a good, tight defence. It's a sin to be lbw but a disgrace to be bowled. There's nothing wrong with failure. Even Bradman, with his world-record Test average of almost 100, had days where he failed. You must analyse your dismissals and learn from the experience, whether it be a first-ball duck or a 99. Carry the memory of that dismissal with you next time you go out.

Think about the possibilities in a game. If rain has fallen, you know running between wickets in anything but spiked shoes is hazardous. Next time it's damp, don't hesitate — put on sprigs, which allow you more balance.

Look around the field before you go in to bat. See who throws right-arm and who throws left-arm. Analyse who are the best, most alert fielders and make a mental note not to take a risk or a sharp run to them.

If you forget how you got out, why you fell over and were run out, or why you got hit for six or dropped a catch, then there's something wrong.

Bowlers know they can't take wickets if they haven't got the ball in their hand. They must always be looking at the captain and be prepared and want to bowl at all times. When you are thrown the ball, believe in yourself, have the confidence to think that you're just one ball away from taking a wicket.

You may have been hit for five fours in a row, but don't think about that. The next one could be mishit and be caught. It mightn't be pretty but it would be out. It could end a big stand, trigger a collapse and help your side win the game.

When Ian Chappell threw me the ball in my first Test, against Pakistan in 1972-73, it was to get a wicket, not because I was taking his sister out or because we were mates. I shared my captain's sentiments, believing I was good enough to get the guy down the other end out.

'When Ian Chappell threw me the ball in my first Test, against Pakistan in 1972-73, it was to get a wicket, not because I was taking his sister out or because we were mates...' Here I dismiss Majid Khan, my second Test wicket; I'm proud of it, even if Majid did make 158!

Your day at the cricket

ONCE THE cricket bug bites you, there's no turning back. You remain an enthusiast for life. I'm just as keen on cricket as ever, even though my playing days are almost over, bar an occasional charity game when time allows.

For months, I'd been meaning to clean out my old work room, but knew once I started, I'd find so many engrossing childhood 'treasures' that it would take the best part of a day to accomplish. Just before Christmas, I gritted my teeth, bolted the door and went for it. Eight hours later I emerged, dusty and dirty but with a huge grin on my face.

It had been one of the most rewarding and pleasurable days I'd had in ages. Among all my old plans, architectural textbooks and papers was a small box, enclosing a set of faded cricket cards and the old pocket scorebook I used down at the TCA Ground in Hobart when the big cricketers came to town.

The cards, from one of those old Scanlon's chewing gum series, featured all my heroes, including Normie O'Neill playing the sweep. At the time, the cards really created a craze! Every cricket-mad kid in our street could be seen walking around chomping on thin bars of pink chewy! It was pretty good stuff, too. But what really got us in were the cricket cards inside the wrappers!

We'd play swaps and have great fun with them. I remember I had to exchange two of Bill Lawry to get one of Normie O'Neill, but it was worth it. We'd take our cards to the cricket, along with our scorebooks, and in impeccable, copperplate writing (we thought it was, anyway!) score the game just like the official scorers up in the grandstand.

I opened my little volume and on the very first page, I'd written down all the names of the 1960-61 West Indians, in batting order, for their game against a Tasmanian XI, bolstered by several 'mainlanders' — Bobby Simpson, O'Neill and Grahame Thomas.

I scored it okay until lunchtime, carefully marking down the dismissals of Cammie Smith, Peter Lashley, Seymour Nurse and Gary Sobers. But then there was a bit of a gap, probably when I went hunting for Wes Hall's autograph and ended up getting the whole team!

I had all sorts of matches in this little book, stretching over a four- or five-year period. It was a real trip down memory lane and as I went from page to page, memories flooded back to me. I could recall where I sat, who I went with, and what sort of day it was. I could almost taste those old tomato sandwiches.

I've included a couple of scoresheets, one for batting and the other for bowling on the following double page so youngsters going to a game can get an idea of how to score. Scoring is pretty simple as long as you remember to do three different steps every time a run is made:

- In the batsman's runs column, mark down the run/runs made;
- Go to the progress score and keep the update going;
- And finally, further down the page, mark the runs against the bowler's name.

If no runs are scored, enter a dot. You have to do pretty small figures. If you leave enough room, you can mark the total number of runs off an over. If it's a maiden over, mark an 'M'.

Take an extra fineliner pen and a tranny with an earpiece so you can listen to the broadcast, in case you have to double check anything. Scorebooks are available from most sporting retailers or specialist cricket shops.

Other than my first cricket bat, I don't think I've had a better present than that old scorebook. It's now out of the old box in the corner and on my shelves in my study, a reminder — along with my autographs — of the day the West Indians came to town!

MATCH   V.

INNINGS.   PLAYED AT   19

	BATSMAN	RUNS	HOW OUT	BOWLER	TOTAL
1					
2					
3					
4					
5					
6					
7					
8					
9					
10					
11					
BYES					
LEG BYES					
WIDE BALLS . . .					
NO BALLS					
			TOTAL FOR INNINGS		

PROGRESS SCORE

Runs at the Fall of each Wicket	1 for	2 for	3 for	4 for	5 for	6 for	7 for	8 for	9 for	10 for	Total

1 2 3 4 5 6 7 8 9 10 11 12 13 14 15 16 17 18 19 20 21 22 23 24 25 26 27 28 29 30
31 32 33 34 35 36 37 38 39 40 41 42 43 44 45 46 47 48 49 50 51 52 53 54 55 56 57 58 59 60
61 62 63 64 65 66 67 68 69 70 71 72 73 74 75 76 77 78 79 80 81 82 83 84 85 86 87 88 89 90
91 92 93 94 95 96 97 98 99 100 101 102 103 104 105 106 107 108 109 110 111 112 113 114 115 116 117 118 119 120
121 122 123 124 125 126 127 128 129 130 131 132 133 134 135 136 137 138 139 140 141 142 143 144 145 146 147 148 149 150
151 152 153 154 155 156 157 158 159 160 161 162 163 164 165 166 167 168 169 170 171 172 173 174 175 176 177 178 179 180
181 182 183 184 185 186 187 188 189 190 191 192 193 194 195 196 197 198 199 200 201 202 203 204 205 206 207 208 209 210
211 212 213 214 215 216 217 218 219 220 221 222 223 224 225 226 227 228 229 230 231 232 233 234 235 236 237 238 239 240
241 242 243 244 245 246 247 248 249 250 251 252 253 254 255 256 257 258 259 260 261 262 263 264 265 266 267 268 269 270
271 272 273 274 275 276 277 278 279 280 281 282 283 284 285 286 287 288 289 290 291 292 293 294 295 296 297 298 299 300
301 302 303 304 305 306 307 308 309 310 311 312 313 314 315 316 317 318 319 320 321 322 323 324 325 326 327 328 329 330

ANALYSIS OF BOWLING

BOWLER	RUNS FOR EACH OVER.	Wide Balls	No Balls	Runs	Wckts	Overs	Maidn Overs	Balls Bwld	Average Runs pr Wicket
	1 2 3 4 5 6 7 8 9 10 11 12								

3

Zootas, flippers and bunnies
(some well-known and not so well-known cricketing terms)

A golden — First-ball dismissal.

Arm ball — A finger spinner's good friend. Instead of spinning normally, the ball tends to drift or swing away. Ideal in trapping the unobservant.

'Aveagoyermug — Get on with it.

Bad trot — A dreaded, unprofitable time for batsmen.

Bat-pad — Close-in catcher, generally sporting a stackhat.

Beamer — Sometimes called a beaner, doodle or a doodlebug. This head-high full toss guaranteed trouble. One from Dennis Lillee at the WACA ground knocked me senseless one day. 'Beetle' Watson got one from Tony Greig at the MCG which cost him pints of blood.

Big Bertha — A big bat; a name given to Bill Ponsford's old bat. Opposing bowlers — and cricket authorities — found it had become too wide, after a chain of big scores. They had to sand it back to fulfil regulations.

Bill Lawry — Bottle opener, indispensable at after-match gatherings.

Bosie — Also known as a googly, a right-arm leg spinner's wrong 'un. Named after Englishman B. J. Bosanquet who confounded batsmen at the turn of the century with his off-breaks bowled with a leg spinner's action.

Bouncer — Bumper, short ball, aimed at unsettling and intimidating batsmen.

Bunny — Batsman who rarely bothers the scorers.

Bunsen burner — Raging turner; a pitch taking a lot of spin.

Castle — A batsman's stumps; furniture.

Chappell 'V' — Hitting the ball in an arc between mid-off and mid-on. Made famous by the Chappell brothers, Ian and Greg, who would eliminate cross bat shots, particularly early in their innings until they became 'set'.

Chatting — Sledging.

Cherry — Six-stitcher, gold Kookaburra, ball.

Chucker — Usually-derogatory term used for bowlers with doubtful actions. There was a host of them in Australia in the late 1950s before the Australian Cricket Board of Control stepped in. The last man to be no-balled in Australasia for throwing in Test cricket was Indian Syed Abid Ali in 1968. Only two Australians have been called for throwing in Test matches — Ernie Jones (1897-98) and Ian Meckiff (1963-64).

Chinaman — The left-arm wrist spinner's googly. It looks like a leg break but instead of spinning into the right hander, it slants away. Only a few bowl it at first-class level. Victorian David Emerson is one. SA's David Hookes also bowls a few. The last Australian I remember taking a wicket in a Test match with a chinaman was Ken Eastwood. This is a good trivia question: who was the batsman? Answer: England's Keith Fletcher.

Cow corner — *See* Slog shot.

Daddles — A duck.

Deck — Wicket, track, pitch.

Doing a Bobby Bitmead — Bowling off the wrong foot.

Doodle — *See* Doodlebug

Doodlebug — *See* Beamer.

Dot ball — A maiden ball.

Double-hopper — one that bounces twice and is usually hit for four. Ask West Indian Roger Harper.

Drop curve — Where a spin bowler beats an advancing batsman with flight, the ball suddenly dropping and making it difficult for the batter to play an attacking shot with safety.

Finger spinner — A right-arm off break bowler, like Brett Henschell (Queensland) or a left-arm orthodox spinner like Paul Jackson (Victoria). SA right-armer Tim May also bowls finger spin, but he tends to give the ball a terrific flick and often tweaks the ball further than the leggies.

Flipper — A wrist spinner's quicker one, which tends to slide through onto the batsmen, often 'back-spinning' and straightening. Even the best players can be caught lbw.

Forty-five — Backward square leg, the halfway point between the wicket-keeper and the square leg umpire. Singles must be saved from here.

Fremantle doctor — Breeze which whips into the WACA ground, providing relief and encouragement for spectators — and seamers who love bowling into it.

French cut — An inside edge wide of the leg stump which generally rockets to the fine leg boundary and raises the temper of even the most placid trundler. Sometimes called the Chinese cut.

Frosty — Cool one, coldie, barbed wire (XXXX), beer.

Gate — Not just the thing you open to get in and off the field, but the gap between bat and pad while a shot is being played.

Globe — No score, duck, googie.

Gold Kookaburra — cricket ball, six-stitcher.

Good nut — One which may not necessarily get a wicket, but boy, was the batsman lucky to survive! *See also* Snorter.

Googly — Bosie or wrong 'un. A leg spinner's 'shock' ball, an off-spinner bowled with a leg break action. Wrist spinners bowl them against left-handers hoping they'll come down the wicket to drive, mis-read the spin and be stranded.

Good line — Bowlers aiming the ball at or just outside off stump.

Good track — Perfect batting wicket; enjoyable for batsmen, not for bowlers.

Gozunda — Grubber; submarine ball, one which hardly rises at all. Almost impossible to stop if they pitch on the stumps.

Holiday resort — Yorker (as in Majorca).

In-dipper — In-swinging delivery; in-ducker. Bruce Reid has a beauty.

Jaffa — The perfect delivery, great nut, pearler.

King pair — Falling first-ball in each innings. Not a pleasant experience, for even the bunnies.

Kuala Lumpur — Bumper.

Lightning — Malcolm Marshall off his long run.

Long hop — Short delivery which balloons at an easy-to-hit height; gift delivery, guaranteed to make your captain wince.

Maiden over — Six deliveries in a row which the batsmen can't score from.

Nelson — All the ones — 111. In England it's considered an unlucky number; the Australian equivalent is 87, 13 short of a century.

Nick — Very fine edge which carries through to the 'keeper for a regulation catch.

Nightwatchman — A lower-order batsman who goes in late in the day to help 'protect' the upper order from batting that night. Usually renowned for his stern defence and resolution, rarely for his smiting or straight hitting.

One fingeree — Also 'uno fingari' or 'fine Italian gentleman'. *See* Arm ball.

On the gully line — Deepish gully, saving one.

Out-dipper — Out-swinger; a delivery which swings away from the right-handers. Very dangerous delivery, depending on what team you represent.

Pair — Out for 0 in both innings.

Pearler — *See* Jaffa.

Popping crease — The line which bowlers are required to deliver from on match days. They generally ignore it at practice.

Rocket arm — Craig McDermott

Rubbish — Bad, easy-to-hit, gift bowling; lollipops.

Sandshoe crusher — A yorker right on or outside leg stump, made famous by Jeff Thomson who used to aim them regularly at Tony Greig's size 14s, thinking the big fellow couldn't get down to them in time.

Silly point — A position reserved only for the unmarried blokes.

Skip — Captain; the bloke you should watch all the time in the field in case he asks you to have a trundle.

Slipper — Close-in slips fieldsman responsible for taking nicks which fly wide of the wicket-keeper.

Slogger — Big-hitter.

Slog shot — The big tonk wide of mid-on, over the head of mid-wicket.

Snorter — Ripper of a delivery; one which does something unusual like swinging in with the arm and cutting away viciously towards the slips. Dennis Lillee used to bowl them regularly.

Stackhat — Helmet.

Stick — Bat.

Sticky wicket — Wet, drying wicket which promotes awkward bounce. The use of covers now restricts the numbers of 'stickies' top-class batsmen have to confront. Club batsmen have to play on them all the time, especially early in the season.

Stumper — Wicket-keeper.

Stumps — Close; end of play; time when the serious drinking often begins.

Suicide — Standing at short leg when Ian Botham is crunching them.

Sweeper — Outrider; boundary fieldsman generally noted for a strong arm, good judgement and good hearing, so he can obey his skipper's demands! The best boundary riders in world cricket today include Australian Mike Veletta, Indian Mohammad Azharuddin and England's Allan Lamb.

The 'Gabba — The Brisbane Cricket Ground, at Woollongabba.

The 'Gee — Melbourne Cricket Ground (MCG).

Thoroughbreds and Clydesdales — Fielders of various skills. The slippers mock the Clydesdales, who in turn, think the slippers are posers and shirkers of hard work in the outfield.

Tom Nix — Six.

Ton — Century; hundred runs.

Trundle — Bowl.

Tweaker — Slow bowler.

Umbrella field — A ring of fieldsman around the batsman, used mainly when fast bowlers are taking the new cherry and are at their liveliest.

Yorker — A well-up delivery, which pitches on or near the batting crease and slips underneath the bat before the batsman is halfway through his down stroke. Craig McDermott has a ripper. Bruce Reid's swinging yorkers are also very hard to handle.

Zoota — A leg spinner's flipper, or fast skimmer, which tends to nip back fast and low into the right-handers. Dangerous delivery perfected by Richie Benaud. Sri Lankan Malcolm Francke boasted that his zoota would get anyone out.

Sri Lankan-born fitness nut Malcolm Francke claimed his zoota could get anyone out.

Acknowledgements

I AM most appreciative to many friends for helping me with the preparation of this book. The photographic departments of the Melbourne *Age* newspaper and *Cricketer* magazine were particularly helpful. Some of Patrick Eagar's photography is truly stunning.

I thank photographer Aldo Marcolin for taking the photo series of Dean Jones and Dean for his permission to use them.

My thanks also to WEG for preparing several of the cartoons inside, Charlie Wat for some of the statistical research and to Ken Piesse for his enthusiasm and expert editorial assistance.

Most of all I thank all my cricket friends around the country — particularly the 'boys' from the Test teams of the '70s, who provided me with so much encouragement.

Bibliography

IT'S IMPOSSIBLE to write a decent cricket book without referring to back editions of the cricketers' bible, *Wisden Cricketers' Almanack*. Old issues of *Cricketer*, *Cricketer Annual* and *Cricket Year Annual* have also helped me to re-check detail and it was great fun rummaging through old *Cricketer* magazine photo files for some 'blasts from the past'.

Other books I have used include *Chappelli* by Ian Chappell (Hutchinson Publishing Group, 1976); *The Wisden Book of Cricket Records*, compiled and edited by Bill Frindall (Macdonald Futura, 1981); *The Doug Walters Story*, by Doug Walters as told to Ken Laws (Rigby Publishers, 1981); *Frindall's Score Book, Australia v West Indies 1975-76* (Lonsdale Universal Limited, 1976); *The Nissan Book of Test Cricket Lists*, compiled by Graeme Atkinson, Graham Dawson and Alan Boardman (The Five Mile Press, 1982); *Bradman and the Bush*, by Ken Piesse and Ian Ferguson (Newspress, 1985); *Australian Cricket: The Game and the Players*, by Jack Pollard (Hodder & Stoughton, 1982); *Cricket Crusader*, by Gary Sobers (Pelham Books, 1966); and *Cricket Glossary '69*, (Test & County Cricket Board, 1969).

For the record

Name: Maxwell Henry Norman Walker.
Born: 12 September 1948 at West Hobart.
State: Victoria.
First-class career: 1968-69 to 1981-82.
Test debut: 1972-73 versus Pakistan (MCG).

Sheffield Shield record:

Batting: 62 matches, 96 innings, 18 not outs, 890 runs, highest score 52, average 11.41, one half-century. 25 catches.
Bowling: 15,011 balls, 6476 runs, 220 wickets, average 29.94, five wickets in an innings 11 times, best bowling 6 for 49.

Test record:

Batting: 34 matches, 43 innings, 13 not outs, 586 runs, highest score 78 (not out), average 19.53, one half-century. 12 catches.
Bowling: 10,094 balls, 3792 runs, 138 wickets, average 27.47, five wickets in an innings 6 times, best bowling 8 for 143.
First Test wicket: Saeed Ahmed (Pakistan).
Last Test wicket: Geoffrey Boycott (England).
Most dismissed batsman: Tony Greig (England) 9 times.
Tours: **For Australia:** West Indies 1972-73, New Zealand 1973-74, England 1975, New Zealand 1976-77, England 1977. **Others:** D. H. Robins to South Africa 1974-75, International Wanderers to South Africa 1975-76.
Best series: 1972-73 versus West Indies — 26 wickets at 20.73 (record number of wickets for Australia versus the West Indies in West Indies).

WSC 'Supertest' record:

Batting: 7 matches, 13 innings, 4 not outs, 158 runs, highest score 30, average 16.55. 3 catches.
Bowling: 1528 balls, 712 runs, 28 wickets, average 25.43, best bowling 7 for 88.
Tours: New Zealand 1978-79, West Indies 1979.
Best series: 1977-78 versus West Indies and the World XI — 26 wickets at 23.70.

Best performances:

Best performance for Australia: **Batting:** 78 not out versus England (the Oval) 1977. **Bowling:** 8 for 143 versus England (MCG) 1974-75.
Best performance for Victoria: **Batting:** 53 versus New Zealanders (MCG) 1973-74 and 52 versus Western Australia (MCG) in the 1972-73 Sheffield Shield season. **Bowling:** 6 for 49 versus South Australia (Adelaide) 1975-76.
Most successful ground in Tests: MCG: 23 wickets at 33.00 and SCG: 23 wickets at 21.43.
Best performance for Australia in WSC: 7 for 88 versus WSC World XI, Sydney Showgrounds, 1977-78.

Hooked on Cricket

Maxwell Henry Norman Walker.
Age: 40 (Born 12/9/48).
Occupation: My son Tristan often asks me this and it's hard to define. I am a television sports presenter, after-dinner speaker, writer and very occasional mid-week cricketer.
Residence: Melbourne.
Major interests: Still photography (I've got a zappy little Minolta); videos; stamp collecting; antiques; reading good biographies.

Cricket career particulars:

Height: Six foot, three and seven-eighths inches (193 cm).
Playing weight: About 14 stone 12 pounds (94 kg). I got back pretty close to this weight for the 1988 Centenary Test revival games.
First clubs: Lansdowne Crescent State School, Friends' School, North Hobart (Under-17s), Liquor Trades XI (a mid-week team open to all publicans and their sons).
Boyhood heroes: Wesley Hall, Ian 'Redders' Redpath, Normie O'Neill.
Personal highlight: Being picked to play for Australia and then staying in the team for almost 10 years. We became the best cricket team in the world and I was proud to be a part of it.
Most memorable moments: 1. Slipping one past Tony Greig and onto his middle stump during the Centenary Test at Melbourne in '77. Bay 13 went berserk and so did I. Modesty prevents me from describing the ball but it did everything and better players than Greigy would have missed it!
2. Dismissing Lawrence Rowe, the 'Black Bradman' on his home deck at Sabina Park in the opening Test of the 1972-73 tour. He'd started his career with 214 and 100 not out on debut against New Zealand at the same ground exactly 12 months earlier and was batting like a train when I got an in-swinger to go. It jagged away on pitching, caught the edge of his bat and Keith Stackpole took the catch at slip.
3. Coming from the clouds to win the third Test at Trinidad during that West Indian tour was also marvellous, probably the biggest team thrill considering we just hadn't looked like winning.
Worst injury: Suffering a broken cheekbone, compliments of my fast bowling pal Dennis Lillee in Perth back in 1975-76. It not only hurt but it dented my ego. I was in good form, too, having made five not out and looking in quite good shape for a big score. The fast bowlers' 'union' was in existence at the time, but Dennis must have felt I looked like a batsman and was entitled to a bouncer. I should, therefore, take it as a compliment. I lost count of the x-rays I had to endure and was in hospital for a good 24 hours.
My only real worries before that had been groin injuries. I broke down in the second Test against New Zealand in Sydney in 1973-74, didn't play again that summer, and had to put up with all sorts of nasty cortisone injections.
Previously, on the very first Saturday of the 1969-70 season — five days after playing in Melbourne's night football premiership — I tore my groin muscles while halfway through my first over for Melbourne against South Melbourne. I missed the whole of that season and the first four games of the '70 footy season as well.
Most embarrassing moments: 1. Being hit by Clive Lloyd for 20 runs in four balls in a WSC one-dayer before the lights went out at VFL Park in 1978-79.
2. Baring my bottom at Nottinghamshire and not knowing it (*see* 'Bottoms up').
3. Having 18 runs taken off three balls by a bloke playing for the Waterside Workers against the Liquor Trades in a mid-week match. They were all snicks and the ground was tiny

but I'd taken something like 5 for 0 before he came in. I did get him out fourth ball but it was an expensive wicket!

Favourite grounds: The 'Gee, my beloved Melbourne Cricket Ground, when it's filled to the brim. I was adopted by Bay 13 and I loved them as much as they loved me. The extra energy they triggered inside of me was amazing. I'll never forget their roars of delight at the Centenary Test when Dennis Lillee got six wickets and I took four to bowl England out for 95. I love Sydney too — especially the 'old' Sydney Cricket Ground — with its ancient stands. The historic, grand pavilion remains a reminder of an earlier era and living proof of what a cricket ground really should look like.

Most admired opponents: 1. In Australia: The Chappell brothers, Ian and Greg, were certainly the toughest batsmen to dislodge. They must have made thousands of runs against Victoria and knocked up scores of centuries. They were both fierce competitors and terrific contributors at Sheffield Shield and Test level.

2. Overseas: West Indian Clive Lloyd played cricket the way it was designed. He had God-given gifts and was a humble champion. A charismatic batsman, he hit the ball hard and often. If the situation demanded it, however, he could also defend and be very hard to dig out.

People I owe most to in cricket: My Dad, Big Max, for making me aware of what sport was all about; Clive Fairbairn at Melbourne for having the foresight to realise that a then-gangly Tasmanian who fancied himself as a batsman was actually a bit of a chance as a fast-medium bowler. He stuck with me, too, even though Jack Potter and Fitzroy took 40 runs from my first five overs on my first XI debut! Clive also knew where best I could bat. I'd come to the club after making successive centuries at No. 3 for North Hobart but Clive immediately put me down at No. 10 where I made a first-ball duck. Even when I graduated to MCC captain, I don't think I batted too much higher!

If I could do something over again: I'd go back and play six more games with Melbourne Football Club and reach the 100-game milestone. While doing this I'd also like to play in a grand final but I was a little unlucky — when I played, there weren't 19 other blokes good enough to get me into a grand final!

I was very fortunate with my cricket, playing with some magnificent blokes. We had a real bond and still do. I made the most of my limited ability and had a ball in the process.

Greatest cricketing friend: I made a wide range of friends from sport and they are all over Australia. The cricketers from the 1970s remain very close. Playing in so many wins brings you closer together and we immediately recaptured that close feeling during the 'revival' Australia—England games in 1988. It was funny. All of us — even Dennis Lillee — found that the Poms weren't half-bad blokes!

Opinions:

The best team of my time: The 1974-75 Australians when we won the Test series 5-1 against England. In batting order: Ian Redpath, Rick McCosker, Ian Chappell, Greg Chappell, Ross Edwards, Doug Walters, Rod Marsh, yours truly, Dennis Lillee, Ashley Mallett, Jeff Thomson.

The best cricketer currently playing: Pound for pound, Viv Richards. When he really tunes in he can still do it. He's a marvellous player and has few peers in the field, too, even at the age of 35.

Favourite current player: Merv Hughes. He's fast becoming one of the most successful and he's still learning, and when you can hear anything from behind that huge, whiskery verandah of his, he talks good sense. Merv's different; one of the game's real characters.

The best team I ever played with — the 1974-75 side at Adelaide. Back row, from left: Dougie Walters, Jeff Thomson, Dennis Lillee, yours truly, Ashley Mallett, Rick McCosker, Terry Jenner. Front row: Rod Marsh, Ian Redpath, Ian Chappell, Ross Edwards and Greg Chappell.

One of my favourite current players, Merv Hughes can be genuinely fast and is a great cricket character.

Today's game: The world's shrunk. Once it would take a couple of months to reach England by boat. Now you can do it in less than 24 hours. More top-class Test cricket is played. At one time, you couldn't afford to miss a game as matches were just too valuable and once out of the side, it'd be tough to get back in. Nowadays, there's so much match play, it doesn't really matter. There's always another big game around the corner. Kids are just as keen as they ever were. The ones who advance are the ones whose ambition shines the brightest. Allan Border has been a marvel, a backbone of steel to this Australian team and when he finally calls it quits, the loss will be considerable — a little like the Australian team in the immediate years after Greg Chappell, Dennis Lillee and Rod Marsh all retired together.